Christopher West

Theology of the Body
For Beginners

ASCEN PRE

West Chester, Pennsylvania

Nihil obstat: Rev. Msgr. Francis A. Barszczewski, STL
Censor Librorum
July 1, 2004

Imprimatur: +Justin Cardinal Rigali
Archbishop of Philadelphia
July 2, 2004

All Scripture quotations are taken from the *Revised Standard Version* of the Bible, copyright 1946, 1952, and 1971 by the Division of Christian Education of the National Council of Churches of Christ in the USA. Used by permission.

Ascension Press
Post Office Box 1990
West Chester, PA 19380
Orders: 1-800-376-0520
www.ascensionpress.com

Cover design: Kinsey Caruth

Printed in the United States of America

ISBN 1-932645-34-9

TABLE OF CONTENTS

LIST OF ABBREVIATIONS

CCC *Catechism of the Catholic Church*, second edition (Libreria Editrice Vaticana, 1997)

DV *Dominum et Vivificantem*, John Paul II's encyclical letter on the Holy Spirit (Pauline, 1986)

EV *Evangelium Vitae*, John Paul II's encyclical letter on the Gospel of Life (Pauline, 1995)

FC *Familiaris Consortio*, John Paul II's apostolic exhortation on the Christian Family (Pauline, 1981)

FR *Fides et Ratio*, John Paul II's encyclical letter on Faith and Reason (Pauline, 1998)

GS *Gaudium et Spes*, Vatican II's Pastoral Constitution on the Church in the Modern World (Pauline, 1965)

HV *Humanae Vitae*, Pope Paul VI's encyclical letter concerning Human Life (Pauline, 1968)

LF *Letter to Families*, John Paul II's letter in the Year of the Family (Pauline, 1994)

LR *Love & Responsibility*, Karol Wojtyla's (John Paul II's) philosophical work on sexuality (Ignatius Press, 1993)

MD *Mulieris Dignitatem*, John Paul II's apostolic letter on the Dignity and Vocation of Women (Pauline, 1988)

NMI *Novo Millennio Ineunte*, John Paul II's apostolic letter at the Close of the Jubilee Year (Pauline, 2001)

OL *Orientale Lumen*, John Paul II's apostolic letter on the Light of the East (Pauline, 1995)

RM *Redemptoris Missio*, John Paul II's encyclical letter on the Mission of the Redeemer (Pauline, 1990)

RH *Redemptor Hominis*, John Paul II's encyclical letter on the Redeemer of Man (Pauline, 1979)

SE *Springtime of Evangelization:* John Paul II's 1998 *ad limina* addresses to the Bishops of the United States (Basilica Press, 1999)

VS *Veritatis Splendor*, John Paul II's encyclical letter on the Splendor of Truth (Pauline, 1993)

WH *Witness to Hope*, George Weigel's biography of Pope John Paul II (HarperCollins, 1999)

Author's Introduction

In January of 2004, *Time* Magazine opened a sixty-page spread on the issue of human sexuality with an article that, even though written from a secular perspective, asked some of the right questions:

> Of all, the splendidly ridiculous, transcendently fulfilling things humans do, it's sex ... that most confounds understanding. What in the world are we doing? Why in the world are we so consumed by it? The impulse to procreate may lie at the heart of sex, but ... bursting from our sexual center is a whole spangle of other things—art, song, romance, obsession, rapture, sorrow, companionship, love, even violence and criminality—all playing an enormous role in everything from our physical health to our emotional health to our politics, our communities, our very life spans.
>
> Why should this be so? Did nature simply overload us in the mating department...? Or is there something smarter and subtler at work, some larger interplay among sexuality, life and what it means to be human? (*Time*, Jan. 19, 2004, p. 64).

This "something smarter at work," that "larger interplay among sexuality, life, and what it means to be human" is precisely what John Paul II explores in great depth and with penetrating insight in his "theology of the body."

The Pope's theology of the body is creating quite a "buzz" in the Church today. In fact, it has already begun what many are calling a "sexual counter-revolution." It's spreading and it can't be stopped. Still, for the vast majority of Christians, the content of the Pope's teaching remains an untapped treasure. Why? As the Pope's biographer George Weigel observes, "The density of John Paul's material is one factor; a secondary literature capable of 'translating' John Paul's [theology of the body] into more accessible categories and vocabulary is badly needed" (WH, p. 343).

My previous book *Theology of the Body Explained*, provides a very thorough, 500-page commentary on John Paul II's revolutionary teaching on the body and sexual love. While that work manages to unfold the Pope's insights and make them more accessible, its sheer size and more academic style can still intimidate the average person. As I wrote in the preface to *Theology of the Body Explained*, smaller-scale efforts are also needed. In response to that need, I humbly present this short introduction.

Those looking for a theologically sophisticated treatment of the Pope's thought should turn to other resources and commentaries. My goal here, as the title indicates, is to simplify John Paul II's theology of the body "for beginners." After laying an important foundation in chapter one, I outline in chapters two through seven the main ideas of the Pope's teaching according to the six-part structure in which he presented it. Chapter eight provides some concluding thoughts on the role of the theology of the body in the "new evangelization." I also include a glossary that not only offers definitions of key terms and phrases for quick reference, but also serves as a summary of the book itself. Finally, the resource section lists organizations that you can contact to learn more about the Pope's theology of the body.

As you proceed, keep in mind that popularizing John Paul II's theology of the body is virtually uncharted territory. Finding the best language, images, and anecdotes with which to do so is a difficult task and remains a work in progress. While my goal, of course, is to convey the essentials of the Pope's teaching, I can't help but deliver it through my own filter. I, like every interpreter of the Pope's work, bring my own personal perspectives, gifts, and shortcomings to the table. As St. Paul says, "test everything; hold fast to what is good" (1 Thess 5:21).

I pray that this book helps to open a new world for you. Indeed, if we take John Paul II's "sexual revolution" to heart, we will never see ourselves and the universe quite the same way again.

—Christopher West
April, 2004

Chapter 1

WHAT IS THE THEOLOGY OF THE BODY?

God "impressed his own form on the flesh ... in such a way that even what was visible might bear the divine form."
—CCC, n. 704

"Theology of the body" is the working title Pope John Paul II gave to the first major teaching project of his pontificate. In 129 short talks delivered between September of 1979 and November of 1984, the Pope offered the Church and the world a rich, biblical reflection on the meaning of human embodiment, particularly as it concerns sexuality and erotic desire.

Catholic theologian George Weigel describes John Paul II's theology of the body as "one of the boldest reconfigurations of Catholic theology in centuries"—"a kind of *theological time-bomb* set to go off with dramatic consequences ... perhaps in the 21st century." At this point the Pope's vision of sexual love "has barely begun to shape the Church's theology, preaching, and religious education." But when it does, Weigel predicts, "it will compel a dramatic development of thinking about virtually every major theme in the Creed" (WH, pp. 336, 343, 853).

God, Sex, & the Meaning of Life

Why might the Pope's study of sexual love impact "every major theme in the Creed"? Because sex isn't just about sex. The way we understand and express

1

our sexuality points to our deepest-held convictions about who we are, who God is, the meaning of love, the ordering of society, and even the ordering of the universe. Hence, John Paul II's theology of the body is much more than a reflection on sex and married love. Through the lens of marriage and the "one flesh" union of spouses the Pope says we rediscover "the meaning of the whole of existence, the meaning of life" (Oct. 29, 1980).*

Christ teaches that the meaning of life is to love as he loves (see Jn 15:12). One of the Pope's main insights is that God inscribed this vocation to love as he loves *in our bodies* by creating us male and female and calling us to become "one flesh" (see Gn 2:24). Far from being a footnote in the Christian life, the way we understand the body and the sexual relationship "concerns the entire Bible" (Jan. 13, 1982). It plunges us into "the perspective of the whole Gospel, of the whole teaching, in fact, of the whole mission of Christ" (Dec. 3, 1980).

Christ's mission is to restore the order of love in a world seriously distorted by sin. And the union of the sexes, as always, lies at the basis of the human "order of love." Therefore, what we learn in the Pope's theology of the body is obviously "important in regard to marriage and the Christian vocation of husbands and wives." However it "is equally essential and valid for the understanding of man in general: for the fundamental problem of understanding him and for the self-comprehension of his being in the world" (Dec. 15, 1982).

---

*Quotes from John Paul II's theology of the body will be referenced by the date of the address. Please note that the 1997 one-volume edition, *The Theology of the Body: Human Love in the Divine Plan* (Pauline), was edited and may differ slightly from the original Vatican edition quoted in this book.

No wonder we're all so interested in sex! The union of the sexes is a "great mystery" that takes us—if we stay the course in our journey of exploration—into the heart of God's plan for the cosmos (see Eph 5:31-32).

Christianity Does Not Reject the Body

When it comes to religion, people are used to an emphasis on the spiritual realm. However, many people are unfamiliar, and sometimes even uncomfortable, with an emphasis on the body. For John Paul II, this is a false divide. Spirit certainly has priority over matter. Yet the *Catechism of the Catholic Church* teaches that "As a being at once body and spirit, man expresses and perceives spiritual realities through physical signs and symbols" (n. 1146). As bodily creatures, this is in a certain sense the only way we *can* experience the spiritual world—in and through the physical world, in and through our bodies. By taking on a body through the *Incarnation*, God humbly meets us right here—in our physical, human state.

Tragically, many Christians grow up thinking of their bodies (especially their sexuality) as inherent obstacles to the spiritual life. Many think Christian teaching considers their spirits to be "good" and their bodies to be "bad." Such thinking couldn't be further from an authentic Christian perspective! The idea that the human body is "bad" is actually a *heresy* (a blatant error explicitly condemned by the Church) known as Manichaeism.

Mani (or Manichaeus), after whom this false teaching is named, condemned the body and all things sexual because he saw in the material world the source of evil. As Christians we believe everything God created is "very good" (see Gn 1:31). John Paul II summarizes the essential distinction as follows: If the Manichaean mentality places an "anti-value" on the body and sexuality, Christianity teaches that the body and sexuality "always constitute a 'value not sufficiently appreciated'" (Oct. 22, 1980). In other words, if Manichaeism says "the body is bad," Christianity says "the body is so good that you can't even fathom it."

The problem with our sex-saturated culture, then, is not that it overvalues the body and sex. The problem is that it has failed to see just how valuable the body and sex really are. *Christianity does not reject the body!* In a virtual "ode to the flesh" the *Catechism* proclaims: "'The *flesh* is the hinge of salvation.' We believe in God who is creator of the *flesh*; we believe in the Word made *flesh* in order to redeem the *flesh*; we believe in the resurrection of the *flesh*, the fulfillment of both the creation and the redemption of the *flesh*" (n. 1015, emphasis added).

The Sacramentality of the Body

The Catholic faith, if you haven't already noticed, is a very fleshy, sensual religion. We most intimately encounter God through our bodily senses and the "stuff" of the material world: through bathing the body with water (baptism); anointing the body with oil (baptism, confirmation, holy orders, anointing of the sick); eating and drinking the Body and Blood of Christ (the Eucharist); the laying on of hands (holy orders, anointing of the sick); confessing with our lips (penance); and the unbreakable joining of man and woman in "one flesh" (marriage).

How can we describe the "great mystery" of the sacraments? They are the physical means by which we encounter God's spiritual treasures. In the sacraments, spirit and matter "kiss." Heaven and earth embrace in a union that will never end.

The human body itself is in some sense a "sacrament." This is a broader and more ancient use of the word than we may be used to. Rather than referring to the seven signs of grace that Christ instituted, when John Paul speaks of the body as a "sacrament," he means it is a sign that makes visible the invisible mystery of God. We can't see God. God is pure Spirit. Yet Christianity is the religion of God's self-disclosure. God wants to reveal himself to us. He wants to make his invisible, spiritual mystery visible to us so that we can "see" him. How does he do so?

Most everyone has experienced that deep sense of awe and wonder in beholding a starlit night or a radiant sunset or a delicate flower. In these moments, we are in some way "seeing God" (more accurately, seeing his reflection). "The beauty of creation reflects the infinite beauty of the Creator" (CCC, n. 341). And yet, what is the crown of creation? What more than anything else in God's creation "speaks" of divine beauty? The answer is man and woman and their call to fruitful communion. "God created man in his own image, in the image of God he created him; male and female he created them. And God blessed them and said to them, 'Be fruitful and multiply...'" (Gn 1:27-28).

John Paul II's Thesis

This brings us to the thesis statement of John Paul II's theology of the body. "The body, in fact, and it alone," the Pope says, "is capable of making visible what is invisible: the spiritual and divine. It was created to transfer into the visible reality of the world, the mystery hidden since time immemorial in God, and thus to be a sign of it" (Feb. 20, 1980). In other words, somehow the body enables us to "see" spiritual realities, even the eternal mystery "hidden" in God. How so?

Think of your own reality as a human being. Human nature is both spiritual and physical. We aren't spirits "trapped" in our bodies. The Church has always maintained that we are embodied spirits, or spiritualized bodies. Through the profound union of body and soul in each of us, our bodies *reveal* or "make visible" the invisible reality of our spirits. But the body does even more. Because we're made in God's image, our bodies also make visible something of God's invisible mystery. It's from this perspective that John Paul wants to study the human body—not as a biological organism, but as a *theology*, as a "study of God." The body isn't divine. But it is a "sign" of the divine mystery.

A sign is something that points us to a reality beyond itself and, in some way, makes that transcendent reality present to us. The divine mystery always remains infinitely "beyond"; it can't be reduced to its sign. Yet the sign is indispensable in "making visible" the invisible mystery. As the *Catechism* says, man "needs signs and symbols to communicate .... The same holds true for his relationship with God" (n. 1146).

We must carefully maintain the essential distinction between spirit and matter and (even more) between Creator and creature. Yet, at the same time, we must affirm the profound unity between these realities. Christianity is the religion of God's union with humanity. It's the religion of the Word (who is pure Spirit) made flesh! In "the body of Jesus 'we see our God made visible and so are caught up in love of the God we cannot see' " (CCC, n. 477). God's mystery is revealed in human flesh—theology *of the body*. This isn't merely the title of a series of papal talks; this is the very "logic" of Christianity.

If at first it appears odd to speak of the body as a theology, it shouldn't upon further reflection. Think about Christmas. We believe in the mystery of a God who took on human flesh and was born of a woman. As John Paul II says, "Through the fact that the Word of God became flesh, the body entered theology ... through the main door" (April 2, 1980).

The Divine Mystery

Several times already we've spoken of the "divine mystery" or the "mystery hidden in God from all eternity" (see Eph 3:9). What does this mean? In the Christian sense, "mystery" does not refer to some unsolvable puzzle. It refers to the innermost reality of God and to his eternal plan for humanity. These realities are so far beyond anything we can comprehend that all we can really utter is the word "mystery." And yet God is "knowable"—not based on our ability to decipher some divine puzzle—but because God has made himself known.

As the *Catechism* says, "God has revealed his innermost secret: God himself is an eternal exchange of love, Father, Son, and Holy Spirit, and he has destined us to share in that exchange" (n. 221). This key statement summarizes the ultimate mystery of God and the meaning of human existence: love. God *is* love, as the apostle John tells us (see 1 Jn 4:8). Not only because he loves us, but because *within God* the three Persons of the Trinity live an "eternal exchange of love." This "is the central mystery of Christian faith and life. It is the mystery of God in himself. It is therefore the source of all the other mysteries of faith, the light that enlightens them" (CCC, n. 234).

In the Pope's language, God is an eternal *Communion of Persons.* A "common union" (communion) of persons is established to the degree that two (or more) persons mutually "give" themselves to one another in love and service. No explanation of the Trinity suffices. Nonetheless, we can discern from revelation that the Father eternally "begets" the Son by *giving himself* to and for the Son. In turn, the Son (the "beloved of the Father") eternally receives the love of the Father and eternally gives himself back to the Father. The love they share *is* the Holy Spirit who, as we say in the Nicene Creed, "proceeds [eternally] from the Father and the Son."

And here's why we exist: Love, by its nature, desires to expand its own communion. God certainly didn't *need* anyone else. The love of the Trinity is perfect and complete in itself. Yet out of sheer goodness and generosity, God wanted to create a great multitude of other persons to share in his own eternal, ecstatic "exchange of love."

Icon of the Trinity, Image of Christ & the Church

So, once again, when we speak of the invisible "mystery hidden in God from time immemorial" we are speaking of the fact that (1) *God is a communion of love* and (2) we are *destined to share in that exchange.* This two-part "mystery" is what the human body signifies right from the moment of our creation. How so? Precisely through the beauty and mystery of sexual difference and our call to become "one flesh" (see Gn 2:24).

God imprinted in our sexuality the call to participate in a "created version" of his eternal "exchange of love." In other words, God created us male and female so that we could image his love by becoming a sincere gift to each other. This sincere giving establishes a "communion of persons" not only between the sexes but also—in the normal course of events—with a "third" who proceeds from them both. In this way, sexual love becomes an icon or earthly image in some sense of the inner life of the

Trinity. (I don't know about you, but I've never heard the media describe it that way.)

In addition to imaging the Trinity, sexual love is also meant to image the union of God with humanity. Christ's redeeming self-donation is a new outpouring of the Trinity's love on all of creation. The Church receives this love and attempts to reciprocate it. God endowed our bodies as male and female with the sacramental ability to convey this exchange between Christ and the Church. As St. Paul says, quoting from Genesis, "'For this reason a man shall leave his father and mother and be joined to his wife, and the two shall become one flesh.' This is a great mystery, and I mean in reference to Christ and the church" (Eph 5:31-32).

This passage from Ephesians 5 is a key text—perhaps *the* key text—for understanding the body and sexuality "theologically." Christ is the one who left his Father in heaven. He also left the home of his mother on earth. Why? To give up his body for his Bride (the Church) so that we might become "one flesh" with him. Where do we unite bodily with Christ? Most profoundly, in the Eucharist.

When all the confusions are cleared and the distortions are untwisted, the deepest meaning of human sexuality—of our creation as male and female and our call to communion—is "eucharist." John Paul II describes the Eucharist as *"the sacrament of the Bridegroom and of the Bride."* As *the* sacrament of communion, the Pope says that the Eucharist serves in some way "to express the relationship between man and woman, between what is 'feminine' and what is 'masculine'" (MD, n. 26). God created us male and female right from the beginning to live in a "holy communion" that foreshadows *the* Holy Communion of Christ and the Church. In turn, the gift of Christ's body to his Bride (celebrated in the

Eucharist) sheds definitive light on the meaning of man and woman's communion.

I never met my father-in-law; he died before my wife and I met. But I admire him tremendously because of the following story. At Mass the day after his wedding, having just consummated his marriage the night before, he was in tears after receiving the Eucharist. When his new bride inquired he said, "For the first time in my life I understood the meaning of Christ's words, 'This is my body given for you.'"

The Spousal Analogy

Scripture uses many images to describe God's love for humanity. Each has its own valuable place. But both Old and New Testaments use the image of spousal love far more than any other. This is also the image favored by the greatest mystics of the Church.

The Bible begins in Genesis with the marriage of the first man and woman, and it ends in Revelation with another "marriage"—the marriage of Christ and the Church. Spousal theology looks to these nuptial "book ends" as a key for interpreting all that lies between. Through this lens we learn that God's eternal plan is to "marry" us (see Hos 2:19)—to live with us in an eternal exchange of love and communion. Not only that but, pushing the analogy, through this union God wants to "impregnate" our humanity with his divine life. This is a very "earthy" way of speaking, but it isn't merely a metaphor. Representing all of us, a woman who walked this planet once opened herself so profoundly to God's love that she literally conceived divine life in her womb. In this way, as the *Catechism* teaches, Mary perfectly fulfills the spousal character of the human vocation in relation to God (see CCC, n. 505).

And here's what we learn from the Pope's theology of the body: God wanted this eternal "marital plan" to be so plain to us—so obvious to us—that he impressed an image of it in our very being by creating us male and female and calling us to become "one flesh."

The Nature of Analogies

At this point it's important to specify that we use spousal love only as an *analogy* of God's mystery. Analogies always indicate, at the same time, both similarity and substantial (in this case, very substantial) dissimilarity. Without this recognition, there's a danger of inferring too much about divine life, based on human life.

For example, God is *not* a sexual being. The mystery of love and generation in the Trinity is infinitely beyond that of human love and generation. Thus the Eucharist as we have just described it is certainly not a "sexual encounter" as we typically think of that expression. This doesn't mean the analogy of sexual love is just wishful thinking or human projection. *God* is the one who inscribed an image of his own mystery in our humanity by creating us male and female. But this is just the point: We are made in God's image, not he in ours. The *Catechism* states this clearly: "In no way is God in man's image. He is neither man nor woman. God is pure spirit in which there is no place for the difference between the sexes. But the respective 'perfections' of man and woman reflect something of the infinite perfection of God" (n. 370; see also CCC, nn. 42, 239).

If all analogies are inadequate, at the same time John Paul II believes the spousal analogy is the *least* inadequate. Speaking of the communion of man and woman and the life it begets, he states, "In this entire world there is not a more perfect, more complete image of God, Unity and Community. There is no other human reality which corresponds more, humanly speaking, to that divine mystery" (Dec. 30, 1981). As we press into this human reality as an image of the divine reality, we must simply be careful to respect the infinite difference between God and his creatures.

The Body & the Spiritual Battle

If God created the body and sexual union to proclaim his own eternal mystery of love, why don't we typically see them in this profound way? For example, when you hear the word "sex," what generally comes to mind? Is it the "great mystery" of the one-flesh union as a foreshadowing of Christ's union with the Church, or something, shall we say, a little less sacred?

Ponder this for a moment. If the body and sex are meant to proclaim our union with God, and if there's an enemy who wants to separate us from God, what do you think he's going to attack? If we want to know what's most sacred in this world, all we need do is look for what is most violently profaned.

The enemy is no dummy. He knows that the body and sex are meant to proclaim the divine mystery. And from his perspective, *this proclamation must be stifled.* Men and women *must be kept from recognizing the mystery of God in their bodies.* As we shall see more clearly later on, this is precisely the blindness that original sin introduced at the serpent's prompting. But have no fear: Christ came preaching the recovery of sight for the blind! (see Lk 4:18)

For now, the point to keep in mind is that the battle for man's soul is fought over the truth of his body. It is no coincidence that St. Paul follows his presentation of the "great mystery" of the "one flesh" union in Ephesians, chapter five, with the call to take up arms in the cosmic struggle between good and evil in Ephesians, chapter six. As the source of the family and life itself, the union of the sexes "is placed at the center of the great struggle between good and evil, between life and death, between love and all that is opposed to love" (LF, n. 23). Therefore, if we're to win the spiritual battle, the first thing St. Paul says we must do—I kid you not, look it up—is "gird [our] loins with the truth" (Eph 6:14). The theology of the body is John Paul II's clarion call for all men and women to do just that—to gird their loins with the truth that will set them free to love.

The Foundation of Ethics & Culture

The stakes are incredibly high in the cultural debate about the meaning of sex and marital love. As John Paul II observes, the communion of the sexes is "the deepest substratum [or foundation] of human ethics and culture" (Oct. 22, 1980). What does this mean? In short, as sex goes, so go marriage and the family. As marriage and the family go, so goes civilization.

This is why Karol Wojtyla (the future Pope John Paul II) wrote in his book *Love & Responsibility* that confusion about sexual morality "involves a danger perhaps greater than is generally realized: the danger of confusing the basic and fundamental human tendencies, the main paths of human existence. Such confusion must clearly affect the whole spiritual position of man" (p. 66).

Think how intertwined sex is with the very reality of human existence. You simply wouldn't exist without the sexual union of your parents—and their parents before them, and their parents before them, and their parents before them .... Every human being is the end result of thousands upon thousands of indispensable sexual unions. Remove just one sexual union from your family tree, and you wouldn't exist. Nor would anyone else who descended from that union. The world would be a different place. Just as effectively, go back any number of generations and insert one contracepted union into your lineage, and you wouldn't exist. Nor would anyone else who descended from that point on your family tree. The world would be a different place.

When we tinker with God's plan for sex, we're tinkering with the cosmic stream of human existence. The human race—its existence, its balance—is literally determined by who is having sex with whom, and, in what manner. When sexual union is oriented towards love and life, it builds families and, in turn, cultures that live the truth of love and life. When it is oriented against love and life, the sexual act breeds death—what John Paul II grimly, yet accurately, describes as a "culture of death." A "culture of death" is a culture that, failing to recognize the infinite worth of every human person, *chooses* death as a "solution" to its problems.

Reclaiming the Truth About Sex

Is the connection between our sexual choices and the culture of death still unclear? Ask yourself: Why do we kill approximately 4,000 unborn babies every day in the United States alone? Because we are misusing and abusing God's great gift of sex. Make no mistake: in the final analysis the abortion debate is not about when life begins. It is about the meaning of sex. What most men and women who fight for abortion want is not so much the "right" to kill their offspring, but the "right" to have unrestricted sex without consequences.

This is why John Paul II wrote in his landmark encyclical *Evangelium Vitae* (*The Gospel of Life*): "It is an illusion to think we can build a true culture of human life if we do not ... accept and experience sexuality and love and the whole of life according to their true meaning and their close inter-connection" (n. 97).

Such logic doesn't bode well for our culture. It's no exaggeration to say that the task of the 20th century was to rid itself of the Christian sexual ethic. If we're to build a "culture of life," the task of the 21st century must be to reclaim it. But the often repressive approach of previous generations of Christians—usually silence or, at most, the incomplete "don't do it" mantra—is largely responsible for the cultural jettisoning of the Church's teaching on sex. We need a "new language" to break the silence and reverse the negativity. We need a fresh theology that explains how the Christian sexual ethic— far from being the prudish list of prohibitions it's often assumed to be—corresponds perfectly with the deepest yearnings of our hearts for love and union.

This is why John Paul II devoted the first major teaching project of his pontificate to developing the theology of the body. A return to God's original plan for the union of the sexes is the only adequate starting point for building a culture that respects the meaning and dignity of human life. But before we dive into the content of the Pope's teaching, we should look briefly at his basic method and approach.

The Pope's Method & Approach

In contrast to more traditional approaches that emphasize the objective categories of "being" and "existence," John Paul II's philosophical approach begins with human experience. He believes that if what the Church teaches is objectively true, then human experience—subjective as it is—should offer confirmation of that truth. Knowing that the Church's message "is in harmony with the most secret desires of the human heart" (CCC, n. 2126), the Pope doesn't need to nor does he attempt to force assent to his proposals. Rather, he invites men and women to reflect honestly on their own experience of life to see if it confirms his proposals.

Those who have been turned off by judgmental moralizers will find this approach delightfully refreshing. The Pope imposes nothing and wags a finger at *no one.* He simply reflects lovingly on God's Word and on human experience in order to demonstrate the profound harmony between them. Then, with utmost respect for our freedom, he invites us to embrace our own dignity. It doesn't matter how often we've settled for something less. This is a message of sexual healing and redemption, not condemnation.

With this compassionate approach—the Gospel approach—John Paul shifts the discussion about sexual morality from *legalism* to *liberty.* The legalist asks, "How far can I go before I break the law?" Instead, the Pope asks, "What's the truth about sex that *sets me free* to love?" In short, through an in-depth reflection on the Scriptures, especially the words of Jesus, John Paul II's theology of the body seeks to answer two universal questions: "What does it mean to be human?" and "How am I supposed to live my life in a way that brings true happiness?" These questions frame the two main parts of the Pope's study. In turn, each of these two parts contains three "cycles" or subdivisions broken down as follows.

In order to understand who we are as male and female, we must look at the three "levels" or "stages" of the human drama:

- Cycle 1: *Our Origin.* This concerns the human experience of sexual embodiment before sin. It is based on Christ's discussion with the Pharisees about God's plan for marriage "in the beginning" (see Mt 19:3-9).

- Cycle 2: *Our History.* This concerns our experience of sexual embodiment affected by sin yet redeemed in Christ. It is based on Jesus' words in the Sermon on the Mount regarding adultery committed "in the heart" (see Mt 5: 27-28).

- Cycle 3: *Our Destiny.* This concerns the human experience of sexual embodiment in the resurrection. It is based on Christ's discussion with the Sadducees regarding the body's glorified state (see Mt 22: 23-33).

Then, in addressing how we are to live, John Paul II looks at the two primary Christian vocations and the issue of sexual morality:

- Cycle 4: *Celibacy for the Kingdom.* This is a reflection on Christ's words about those who sacrifice marriage for the kingdom of heaven (see Mt 19:12).

- Cycle 5: *Christian Marriage.* This is primarily a reflection on St. Paul's grand "spousal analogy" in Ephesians 5.

- Cycle 6: *Love and Fruitfulness.* This re-examines the Christian sexual ethic in light of the entire preceding analysis, giving fresh insight into the nature of sexual love and procreation.

The chapters that follow will introduce you to the main themes of these six cycles.

Chapter 2

Before The Fig Leaves: God's Original Plan For The Body And Sex

"This is the body: a witness ... to Love."
—John Paul II (Jan. 9, 1980)

If you've ever read anything John Paul II has written, you've certainly encountered one of his favorite passages from the Second Vatican Council: "Jesus Christ ... by the revelation of the mystery of the Father and his love fully reveals man to himself and makes his supreme calling clear" (GS, n. 22). This is John Paul's anthem: Christ "fully reveals" what it means to be human. Thus, even though his goal in this cycle is to reflect on God's original plan for the sexes as found in the book of Genesis, the Pope begins with the words of Christ. Genesis, in fact, can only be fully understood in the light of Christ.

In the Beginning it Was Not So

When some Pharisees questioned Jesus about the meaning of marriage, they recalled to him that Moses allowed divorce. Jesus' reply provides one of the keys to understanding the Gospel: "For your hardness of heart Moses allowed you to divorce your wives, but from the beginning it was not so" (Mt 19:8). In effect, Jesus is saying something like this: "Do you think all the tension, conflict, and heartache in the male-female relationship is

19

normal? This isn't normal. This isn't the way God created it to be. Something has gone terribly wrong."

Here's an image I like to use to bring this home. It's as if we're all driving around town in cars with flat tires. The rubber is shredding off the rims; the rims are getting all dented up; and we just think this is normal. After all, everyone's tires look this way. According to the analogy, Jesus is saying to the Pharisees (and to all of us), "In the beginning, they had air in their tires."

So, if we want to know the meaning of the "one flesh" union, according to Christ, we have to go back to "the beginning," before sin distorted things. That's the standard. That's the norm. As we look at John Paul II's reflections on the creation texts, we will probably realize at a new level just how far we've all fallen from God's plan. But don't despair! Christ came into the world not to condemn those with flat tires. He came into the world to re-inflate our flat tires. We can't actually return to the state of innocence—we've left that behind. But by following Christ we can receive God's original plan for the sexes and live it with Christ's help (see CCC, n. 1615).

Original Human Experiences

John Paul takes a refreshing look at the creation stories. Rather than looking abstractly at God's original plan, the Pope wants to consider the first man and woman's *experiences* of the body and sexuality. We, of course, don't have any direct experience of the first man and woman's state of total innocence. Nonetheless, the Pope proposes that an "echo" of the beginning exists within each of us. The original human experiences, he says, "are always at the root of every human experience .... They are, in fact, so intermingled with the ordinary things of life that we do not generally notice their extraordinary character" (Dec. 12, 1979).

We approach these experiences through "the symbolism of biblical language" (CCC, n. 375). Symbolism is the most apt way to convey deep spiritual truths, which is what Genesis seeks to do. We needn't get hung up on the modern assertion that science has "disproved" the creation stories in Genesis. The creation stories were never meant to be scientific accounts of the origin of the world. Scientific knowledge is certainly valuable as far is it goes, but it can't tell us the spiritual *meaning* of our existence. For this, the divinely inspired authors of Scripture employed the symbolism with which we are familiar.

Here's an analogy. Consider the difference for a woman when her optometrist looks in her eyes and when her husband or boyfriend does so. The scientist is looking at her cornea and records the scientific facts. The lover is looking at her soul and proclaims something more poetic and inspired (we hope). Does the scientist "disprove" the lover? No. These are simply two perspectives on the same reality. The author of Genesis wasn't a scientist, but a lover inspired by God to proclaim the spiritual mysteries at the origin of the world and of mankind. We must keep this in mind as we examine the creation stories.

According to John Paul, three experiences in particular define the human person in the state of innocence: *solitude, unity,* and *nakedness.* Much ink can be spilt unpacking the Pope's profound reflections on these experiences (see my book, *Theology of the Body Explained*). Here, of course, I'm only presenting a basic sketch. As I do, see if you don't find an "echo" of these experiences in your own heart.

Original Solitude: The First Discovery of "Personhood"

"Then the Lord God said, 'It is not good that the man should be alone; I will make him a helper fit for him'" (Gn

2:18). The most obvious meaning of this "solitude" is that the man is alone without woman. But the Pope mines a deeper meaning from this verse. This creation account doesn't even distinguish between male and female until after Adam's "deep sleep." Here Adam represents all of us—men and women (*adam* in Hebrew means "man" in the generic sense). Man is "alone" because he's the only bodily creature made in God's image and likeness. Man is "alone" in the visible world as a *person*.

When Adam names the animals, he also discovers his own "name," his own identity. He was looking for a "helper," but didn't find one among the animals (see Gn 2:20). Adam *differs* from the animals. What does the human person have that the animals don't? In a word, freedom. Adam isn't determined by bodily instinct. He's created from "the dust" like the animals (he's bodily), but he also has the "breath of life" inspiring his body (see Gn 2:7). An inspired body is not just *a* body but *some*body. A *person* can choose what to do with his or her body. Mere dust cannot.

In this freedom Adam experiences himself as a *self*. He's more than an "object" in the world; he's a "subject." He has an "inner world" or an "inner life." It's impossible to speak of the inner life of a squirrel or a chicken. It's precisely this "inner life" that the words "subject" and "person" capture. Despite some modern propaganda to the contrary, we know intuitively that chickens aren't "people too." We owe special respect to all of God's creatures (see CCC, nn. 2415-2418), yet no other bodily creature shares the dignity of being created in God's image.

Why was Adam endowed with freedom? Because Adam was called to love, and without freedom, love is impossible. In his solitude, Adam realizes that love is his origin, his vocation, and his destiny. He realizes that, unlike the animals, he's invited to enter a "covenant of love" with God himself. It is this relationship of love with God that defines Adam's "solitude" more than anything else. Tasting this love, he also longs with all his being to share this love (covenant) with another person like himself. This is why it's "not good for the man to be alone."

In his solitude, therefore, Adam has already discovered his two-fold vocation: love of God and love of neighbor (see Mk 12:29-31). He has also discovered his capacity to negate this vocation. God *invites* Adam to love; he never forces him because *forced* love isn't love at all. Adam can say "yes" to God's invitation, or he can say "no." And this fundamental choice is expressed and realized *in his body.* Solitude—the first discovery of personhood and freedom—is something spiritual, but it is "experienced" bodily. As John Paul says, the "body expresses the person" (Oct. 31, 1979). We can also say, the body expresses the freedom of the person, or, at least it's meant to.

Reclaiming an abused phrase, God is entirely "pro-choice." He gave us freedom in the first place. But some choices negate our vocation to love. Some choices can *never* bring happiness. We *are* "free" in a sense to "do whatever we want with our bodies." However, we're not free to determine whether what we do with our bodies is good or evil. As Adam learned, this is a tree (the "tree of the knowledge of good and evil") from which he cannot eat, lest he die (see Gn 2:16-17). Therefore, human freedom—"choice"—is fully realized not by inventing good and evil, but by choosing properly between them.

All of these insights are "contained" in the experience of Adam's solitude. Freedom is given for love. It can lead to destruction and division, but it's intended to bestow life and establish unity. It's our *choice.*

Original Unity: The Communion of Persons

After Adam named all the animals without finding a lover among them, we can imagine his sentiment upon seeing the woman. Adam's cry, "This at last is bone of my bones and flesh of my flesh!" (Gn 2:23) expresses absolute wonder and fascination.

Notice the bodily focus. Adam is fascinated with *her body* because, as the Pope points out, this "at last" is a body that expresses a person. All the animals he named were bodies, but not persons. We lose this in English, but for the Jews, "flesh" and "bones" signified the whole human being. Hence, woman's creation from one of Adam's bones (see Gn 2:21-22) is a figurative way of expressing that both men and women share the same humanity. Both are persons made in God's image. Both are "alone" in the world in the sense that they are both *different* from the animals (original solitude); both are called to live in a covenant of love.

"Therefore a man leaves his father and his mother and cleaves to his wife, and they become one flesh" (Gn 2:24). This experience of *unity* overcomes man's *solitude* in the sense of being alone without the "other." But it affirms everything about human solitude in the sense that man and woman are both persons different from the animals. The human union in "one flesh" is worlds apart from the copulation of animals. What's the big difference? Admittedly it looks much the same biologically, but human sexual union isn't merely a biological reality. It's also a spiritual and *theological* reality. The human body is meant to reveal and participate in the spiritual mystery of divine love. As the *Catechism* states, "In marriage, the physical intimacy of the spouses becomes a sign and pledge of spiritual communion" (CCC, n. 2360). Animals aren't capable of this "spiritual communion" because they aren't spiritual. Their "dust" or matter isn't "in-spired" (filled with the Spirit). They aren't made in God's image.

Becoming "one flesh," therefore, refers not only to the joining of two bodies (as with animals) but is "a 'sacramental' expression which corresponds to the communion of persons" (June 25, 1980). Recall our discussion on the "sacramentality" of the body. The human body makes visible the invisible mystery of God who himself is an eternal Communion of Persons; of God who himself is love.

Here the Pope presents a dramatic development of Catholic thinking. Traditionally theologians have said we image God as individuals, through our rational soul. This is certainly true. But John Paul II takes it a step further when he states: "Man becomes the image of God not so much in the moment of solitude as in the moment of communion." In other words, man images God "not only through his own humanity, but also through the communion of persons which man and woman form right from the beginning." He even says that this "constitutes, perhaps, the deepest theological aspect of all that can be said about man." Finally, he observes that on "all this, right from the beginning, there descended the blessing of fertility" (Nov. 14, 1979).

God could not have bestowed a greater purpose and dignity on sexual love. As was stated previously, marital union is meant to be an icon in some way of the inner life of the Trinity! If we could take in this one truth and reflect on it, we would never view sex the same way again. God, remember, is not sexual. The earthly image pales in comparison to the divine reality. Nonetheless, God created us as male and female and called us to communion as the primordial (original, fundamental) revelation of his own mystery in the created world. This is what the Pope means when he describes marriage as the "primordial sacrament." The whole reality of married life, of course, is a sacrament. But nowhere is the "great mystery" more evident than when the two become "one flesh."

Original Nakedness: Key to Understanding God's Original Plan

Having discussed the original experiences of *solitude* and *unity*, we are ready to explore the third original experience—*nakedness*.

After the words describing their unity, we read that "the man and his wife were both naked, and were not ashamed" (Gn 2:25). Of all the passages in the creation stories, the Pope says that this one is "precisely the key" for understanding God's original plan for human life. That's a bold assertion. In short, if we don't understand the meaning of Genesis 2:25, we don't understand the meaning of our creation as male and female; we don't understand ourselves and the meaning of life.

But how can we understand original nakedness when we, having inherited the "fig leaves," have no direct experience of it? We do so only by contrast; by looking at our own experience of shame and "flipping it over."

A woman doesn't feel the need to cover her body when she's alone in the shower. But if a strange man burst into the bathroom she would. Why? The Pope proposes that "shame" in this sense is a form of self-defense against being treated as an object for sexual use. In the case of this woman, she knows that she is never, ever meant to be treated as a "thing" for someone's kicks. Experience teaches her that men (because of the lust that resulted from original sin) tend to objectify women's bodies. Therefore, the woman covers her body not because it's "bad" or "shameful." She covers herself to protect her

own dignity from the stranger's "lustful look"—a look
that fails to respect her God-given dignity as a person.

Take this experience of fear (shame) in the presence
of another person, "flip it over" and we arrive at Adam
and Eve's experience of nakedness *without* shame. Lust
(self-seeking sexual desire) hadn't yet entered the
human heart. Hence, our first parents experienced a
total defenselessness in each other's presence because
the other's look posed no threat whatsoever to their
dignity. As John Paul poetically expresses, they "see and
know each other ... with all the peace of the interior gaze"
(Jan. 2, 1980). This "interior gaze" indicates not only the
sight of a body, but a body that reveals a personal and
spiritual mystery. They saw God's plan of love (theology)
inscribed in their naked bodies and *that's exactly what they
desired*—to love as God loves in and through their bodies.
And there is no fear (shame) in love. "Perfect love casts
out fear" (1 Jn 4:18).

This is why "nakedness without shame" is the key for
understanding God's plan for our lives—it reveals the
original truth of love. Let this point sink in: God created
sexual desire "in the beginning" to be the very power
to love as he loves—in a free, sincere, and total gift of
self. *This is how the couple described in Genesis experienced it.*
Sexual desire wasn't felt as a compulsion or instinct for
selfish gratification. The experience of lust comes only
with the dawn of sin. Lust is a result of what we might call
"flat-tire syndrome."

Since the first man and woman were "fully inflated"
with God's love, they were entirely free to be a gift to one
another. They were "free with the very freedom of the
gift," as the Pope puts it (Jan. 16, 1980). Only a person
who is free from the compulsion of lust is capable of
being a true "gift" to another. The "freedom of the gift,"
then, is the freedom to *bless*, which is the freedom from

the compulsion to *grasp* and *possess*. It is this freedom that allowed the first couple to be "naked without shame."

As a result of sin, our experience of sex has become terribly distorted. In the midst of these distortions, we can tend to think that there must be something wrong with sex itself (the "body-bad/sex-dirty" mentality stems from this). But the distortions we know so well are *not* at the core of sex. At the core of sex we discover a sign of God's own goodness. "God saw everything that he had made, and behold, it was very good" (Gn 1:31).

According to John Paul, nakedness without shame demonstrates that the first couple participated in this same vision of God. They *knew* their goodness. They *knew* God's glorious plan of love. They *saw* it inscribed in their bodies and they *experienced* it in their mutual desire. We lost this glorious vision with the dawn of sin. But don't forget that "Jesus came to restore creation to the purity of its origins" (CCC, n. 2336). This won't be complete until heaven, yet through the gift of redemption, we can begin to reclaim what was lost even in this life.

The Nuptial Meaning of the Body

Since lust so often holds sway in our fallen world, nakedness is often intertwined with all that is not holy. But in the beginning, John Paul says it was nakedness that revealed God's holiness in the visible world. God's holiness is his eternal mystery of self-giving love—the "exchange of love" between Father, Son, and Holy Spirit. Human holiness, in turn, is what "enables man to express himself deeply with his own body ... precisely by means of the 'sincere gift' of himself" (Feb. 20, 1980).

Here the Pope draws from another favorite passage from Vatican II: "Man can fully discover his true self only in a sincere giving of himself" (GS, n. 24). In other words, we can only discover "who we are" by loving as God loves. This, of course, is Christ's new commandment: "Love one another as I have loved you" (Jn 15: 12). How did Christ love us? Recall his words at the Last Supper: "*This is my body which is given for you*" (Lk 22:19). Love is supremely spiritual, but as Christ demonstrates, love is expressed and realized *in the body*. In fact, God inscribed the call to divine love in our bodies—in our sexuality—right from the beginning.

In their nakedness, the first man and woman discovered what the Pope calls "the nuptial meaning of the body." Nuptial love (we could also say marital, spousal, or conjugal love) is the love of *total self-donation*. The nuptial meaning of the body, therefore, is the body's "capacity of expressing love: that love precisely in which the person becomes a gift and—by means of this gift—fulfills the very meaning of his being and existence" (Jan. 16, 1980).

If you are looking for the meaning of life, according to John Paul II, it's impressed right in your body—in your sexuality! The purpose of life is to love as God loves, and this is what your body as a man or woman calls you to. Think of it this way: A man's body doesn't make sense by itself. Nor does a woman's body. But seen in light of each other, sexual difference reveals the unmistakable plan of God that man and woman are meant to be a "gift" to one another. Not only that, but their mutual gift (in the normal course of events) leads to a "third." As John Paul expresses it, "knowledge" leads to generation: "Adam *knew* his wife and she conceived" (Gn 4:1).

Fatherhood and motherhood "crown" and completely reveal the mystery of sexuality. God's first directive in Genesis, "Be fruitful and multiply" (Gn 1:28), isn't merely an injunction to propagate. It's a call to love in God's image and thus "fulfill the very meaning of our being and existence."

The Fundamental Element of Existence

Marriage and procreation, of course, aren't the only way to "love as God loves." They serve as the original model, but whenever we imitate Christ in "giving up our bodies" for others, we express the body's nuptial meaning. Christ, in fact, will call some to sacrifice marriage "for the sake of the kingdom" (see Mt 19:12). As we'll see more clearly in chapter 5, celibacy for the kingdom *is not a rejection of sexuality.* It's a call to embrace *the ultimate meaning and purpose of sexuality.* The "one flesh" union is only a foreshadowing of something infinitely more grand and glorious—the eternal union of Christ and the Church (see Eph 5:31-32). Again, this will be clearer later on, but those who choose Christian celibacy "skip" earthly marriage to devote themselves entirely to the eternal one.

Whatever our particular vocation, we're all called to participate in God's love and share it with others. When we have the purity to see it, this is what the human body and human sexuality teach us. The nuptial meaning of the body (that is, the call to love that God inscribed in our flesh) reveals what Vatican II describes as "the universal call to holiness." And yet how many people spurn their bodies and their sexuality in the name of a supposed holiness? The nuptial meaning of the body "is the fundamental element of human existence in the world" (Jan. 16, 1980). We dare not spurn this! The more we grow in authentic (that is, embodied) holiness, the more we "discover and strengthen that bond that exists between the dignity of the human being (man or woman) and the nuptial meaning of his body" (July 21, 1982).

How do we grow in authentic, embodied holiness? How do we begin to reclaim something of the happiness and peace experienced by the first man and woman? The Pope examines this in his next cycle of reflections.

Chapter 3

THE ENTRANCE OF THE FIG LEAVES: THE EFFECTS OF SIN AND THE REDEMPTION OF SEXUALITY

*In the Sermon on the Mount "the Spirit of the Lord gives new form
to our desires, those inner movements that animate our lives"*
—CCC, n. 2764

In his second cycle of reflections, the Pope contemplates the sexual and bodily experiences of "historical" men and women. History, in this sense, begins with the entrance of the fig leaves—that is, with the dawn of sin (see Gn 3:7-10). But, as historical men and women, we're not only affected by sin; we're also redeemed in Christ. We must always balance the "bad news" of sin with the "good news" of redemption.

The bad news, as this chapter will discuss in more detail, is that we've fallen from the purity of our origins. The good news we'll unfold is that "Jesus came to restore creation to the purity of its origins" (CCC, n. 2336). As stated earlier, we can't return to the state of innocence, but by the power of Christ's death and resurrection, we can progress more significantly on the journey of restoration than most people imagine. This can be a "messy" journey. Yet even though the fullness of redemption is reserved for heaven, our flat tires really can regain a significant amount of air even here on earth.

Adultery in the Heart

Once again, the Pope bases his reflections on Christ's words, this time from the Sermon on the Mount: "You have heard that it was said, 'You shall not commit adultery.' But I say to you that everyone who looks at a woman lustfully has already committed adultery with her in his heart" (Mt 5:27-28).

For the sake of example, Christ speaks directly of male lust, but the principle applies equally to women. Most would agree that male lust seems geared more toward physical gratification at the expense of a woman, while female lust seems geared more toward emotional gratification at the expense of a man. Of course, this is not always the case. Women have physical cravings just as men have emotional ones. But the saying that "men will use love in order to get sex and women will use sex in order to get love" rings true at some level.

We can also observe that some people experience lust for the same sex. Homosexuality is a complex issue that we can't discuss at length here. (For a more detailed discussion, see chapter 8 of my book *Good News about Sex & Marriage*.) In short, while there is a strong push today to normalize homosexuality, in reality it's another manifestation of "flat-tire syndrome." No matter what our particular experience of lust, we're all in need of "re-inflation." The good news of the Gospel is that, if we take up our crosses and follow him, Christ can empower all of us to live in accord with God's wise design for creating us male and female. No one—no matter what his or her distortions—is beyond the scope of Christ's redeeming love.

When Christ speaks of "looking with lust," he isn't saying that a mere glance or momentary thought makes us guilty of adultery. As fallen human beings, we'll always be able to sense the "pull" of lust in our hearts and in our bodies. This doesn't mean we've sinned. It's what we do when we experience the pull of lust that matters. Do we seek God's help in resisting it, or do we indulge it? When we indulge it—that is, when we actively choose "in our hearts" to treat another person as merely an object for our own gratification—we seriously violate that person's dignity and our own. We're meant to be loved "for our own sakes," never used as an object for someone else's sake. For John Paul II, the opposite of love isn't hatred; rather, the opposite of love is to *use* someone as a means to our own selfish ends.

Furthermore, it's significant that Christ refers to looking lustfully at "a woman" in the generic sense. He doesn't stress that it's someone other than a spouse. As John Paul observes, a man commits "adultery in the heart" not only by looking lustfully at a woman he isn't married to, "but *precisely* because he looks at a woman in this way. Even if he looked in this way at his wife, he could likewise commit adultery 'in his heart'" (Oct. 8, 1980). In other words, marriage does *not* justify lust. It doesn't make *using* your spouse "okay." I know this is a cliché, but why do so many wives claim to have a "headache" when their husbands want to have sex? If a woman is being *used* by her husband, it's totally understandable for her to recoil. The sexual embrace is meant to image and express divine love. Anything less is a counterfeit that not only fails to satisfy, but wounds us terribly.

Words of Salvation, Not Condemnation

The Pope acknowledges that Christ's words about lust are severe. But he asks, are we to fear the severity of these words, or rather have confidence in their power to save us (see Oct. 8, 1980)? These words have power to save us because the one who speaks them is the "Lamb of God who takes away the sin of the world" (Jn 1:29). Most people see in Christ's words only a condemnation. Do we forget that Christ came into the world not to condemn, but to save (see Jn 3:17)?

Christ's words about lust call us to "enter our full image" (see April 23, 1980). As part of the heritage of original sin, lust obscures in each of us God's original, beautiful plan for sexual love—but it hasn't snuffed it out. The Pope insists that the heritage of our hearts is *deeper* than lust, and if we're honest with ourselves, we still desire what is deeper. If the human heart is a deep well, it's true that murky waters abound. But if we press through the mud and the mire, at the bottom of the well we don't find grime and sludge. We find a spring that, when activated, gradually fills the well to overflowing with pure, living water. This spring is the "deeper heritage" of our hearts. John Paul II proclaims that the words of Christ reactivate that deeper heritage, giving it *real power* in our lives (see Oct. 29, 1980).

This means that we needn't walk through life merely coping with our lusts and disorders. Christ didn't die on a cross and rise from the dead to give us more coping mechanisms for our sins. We already had plenty of those without a savior. Christ died on a cross and rose from the dead so that we, too, could live a new life (see Rom 6:4). Again, we need to stress that this "new life" will only come to fulfillment in the resurrection at the end of time; "but it is also true that, in a certain way, we have already risen with Christ" (CCC, n. 1002). Here and now we can begin to experience the redemption of our sexual desires, the gradual transformation of our hearts. It is a difficult and even arduous journey, but one that can be accomplished.

Questioning God's Gift

If we're to experience the redemption of our sexuality, we must first examine how and why we fell from God's original plan for it. So, once again, John Paul II takes us back to Genesis, this time to examine the nature of the original sin and the entrance of the fig leaves.

The Pope describes original sin as "the questioning of the gift." Allow me to explain. The deepest yearning of the human heart is to be "like God" by sharing in his life and love. Right from the beginning, God had granted man and woman a sharing in his own life and love as a totally free gift. Using the spousal image, God *initiated* the gift of himself as "bridegroom," and man (male and female) opened to *receive* the gift as "bride." In turn, man and woman were able to re-image this same "exchange of love" through their own marital self-giving and unity.

In order to retain this divine likeness and remain in his love, God had only asked that they not eat from "the tree of the knowledge of good and evil." If they did eat of it, they would cut themselves off from the source of life and love. In other words, they'd die (see Gn 2:16-17).

Sounds simple enough. So where did it all go wrong? "Behind the disobedient choice of our first parents lurks a seductive voice, opposed to God, which makes them fall into death out of envy. Scripture and the Church's Tradition see in this being a fallen angel, called 'Satan' or the 'devil'" (CCC, n. 391). As we observed in the first chapter, Satan's no dummy. He knows that God created the union of the sexes as a sharing in divine life, and his goal is to keep us from this. So he aims his attack at "the very heart of that unity, which, from the 'beginning,' was formed by man and woman, created and called to become 'one flesh'" (March 5, 1980).

Having approached the woman—the one who represents us all as "bride" in our *receptivity* to God's gift—the serpent insists, "You will not die [if you eat from the forbidden tree]. For God knows that when you eat of it your eyes will be opened, and you will be like God, knowing good and evil" (Gn 3:4-5). We might read the serpent's temptation like this: "God doesn't love you. He's not lookin' out for you. He's a tyrant, a slave-driver who wants to keep you from what you really want. That's why he told you not to eat from that tree. If you want life and happiness, if you want to be 'like God,' then you have to reach out and grasp it for yourself because God sure won't give it to you."

Herein lies *the questioning*, and ultimately, the denial of God's gift. In the moment they reject their *receptivity* before God and *grasp* at their own "happiness," they turn their backs on God's love, on God's gift. In a way, they cast God's love out of their hearts. "Then the eyes of both were opened, and they knew that they were naked; and they sewed fig leaves together and made themselves aprons" (Gn 3:7).

The tendency to "grasp" seems built-in to our fallen nature. We can observe it even in little children. For example, when my son asks for a cookie for dessert, before I can even get the cookie out of the box to present it to him as a gift, what does he do? He *grasps* at it. So, taking advantage of this teachable moment, I might say to him, "Thomas, you're denying the gift. Your Papa loves you. I want to *give* this cookie to you as a gift. If you believed in the gift, all you would need to do is hold your hands out in confidence and *receive* the cookie as a gift." This is the problem with us all. We don't trust enough in our Father's love, so we grasp at happiness.

The Second Discovery of Sex

God said if they ate from the tree they would die. They didn't keel over dead, but they did die spiritually. In the act of creation, God had "in-spired" their bodies with his own life and love (see Gn 2:7). Now their bodies "ex-spired" ("breathed-out") God's Spirit. Void of God's love, their desire for one another was altogether different. Having "denied the gift" in their relationship with God, they no longer experienced sexual desire as the power to be a gift to one another. Instead, they desired to *grasp* and *possess* one another for their own gratification. As John Paul says, with the dawn of lust, the "relationship of the gift is changed into the relationship of appropriation" (July 23, 1980). To "appropriate" in this sense means "to take hold of" with the desire to *use.*

The Pope calls this "the second discovery of sex." In the "first" discovery of sex they experienced total peace and tranquility. Now they immediately felt "threatened." Nakedness originally revealed their God-like dignity. Now they instinctively hide their nakedness from the other's look.

Shame, therefore, has a double meaning. It indicates that they've lost sight of the nuptial meaning of their bodies (God's plan of love stamped in their sexuality), but it also indicates an inherent need to *protect* the nuptial meaning of the body from the degradation of lust. As the Pope poetically expresses it, lust "passes on the ruins" of the nuptial meaning of the body and aims directly to satisfy only the "sexual need" of the body (see Sept. 17, 1980). It seeks "the sensation of sexuality" apart from a true gift of self and a true communion of persons. Lust, in fact, shatters their communion.

Lust is often thought of as some benefit to the sexual relationship or it is conceived of as an *increase* or *intensification* of sexual desire. In reality, lust is a *reduction* of the original fullness God intended for sexual desire. We don't get "more" when we lust, but much less. Indulging in lust is comparable to eating out of a dumpster, when God invites us to the feast of eternal life. Why would we ever choose a dumpster? Because we don't really believe in the great gift of God's banquet. This is the gift man and woman denied with original sin. Shame, in turn, indicates our attraction toward the "dumpster."

In a way man and woman blame their bodies for lust. But such an approach is quite literally a "cover-up"—almost an "excuse" not to face the deep disorder of their hearts. As Jesus stresses in the Sermon on the Mount, lust is first and foremost a problem of the heart, not the body. Until we address the disordered desires of our hearts, we will never be able to live as the men and women God created us to be. As we observed previously, lust tends to affect the male and female personality differently, but the hearts of both men and women have "become a battlefield between love and lust" (July 23, 1980).

Christian Ethos: Morality "from the Heart"

Conforming our behavior to an external norm isn't enough. We all know it's possible to follow "the rules" without ever attaining holiness (that is, without a heart "in-spired" by God's love). This kind of rigid and lifeless conformity to rules is called "legalism" or "moralism." In the Sermon on the Mount, Christ calls us to something *very* different. He calls us to a "living morality" that flows from the heart.

Jesus sets the stage for this "new" morality by saying, "Unless your righteousness exceeds that of the scribes and the Pharisees, you will never enter the kingdom of heaven" (Mt 5:20). What could these words have sounded like to the Jews who heard them? The Scribes and the Pharisees were considered the most righteous of all. But for many of them, at least the ones Jesus singled out, it was all external. They conformed to the ethic, but their "ethos" remained skewed.

An *ethic* is an external norm or rule—"do this," "don't do that." *Ethos* refers to a person's inner-world of values, what attracts and repulses him deep in the heart. In the Sermon on the Mount, Christ isn't only confirming God's ethical code. He is also proclaiming the true *ethos* of God's commandments—what they call us to *internally*. In effect Christ says, "You've heard the ethic not to commit adultery, but the problem is you *desire* to commit adultery. Your *ethos* is flawed because you're filled with lust."

It seems almost cruel. Knowing we're filled with lust, Jesus says, "Don't lust." Great! So what are we supposed to do? Christ holds out a standard he knows we can't meet. It seems hopeless—*unless* ... unless it were possible to experience some kind of redemption or transformation of our desires. This is precisely where the Gospel becomes *good news*. As John Paul II repeatedly stresses, the "new ethos" that Christ proclaims in the Sermon on the Mount is not only given to us as a task. It's also given as a gift. We aren't left to our own flaws, weaknesses, and sinfulness. In the "Sermon on the Mount ... the Spirit of the Lord gives new form to our desires, those inner movements that animate our lives" (CCC, n. 2764).

As the Pope puts it, "Christian ethos is characterized by a transformation of the conscience and attitudes of ... both man and woman, such as to express and realize the value of the body and sex according to the Creator's original plan" (Oct. 22, 1980). What good news! What hope! What joy! We aren't *bound* by lust. "The new dimension of *ethos* is always connected with ... liberation from 'lust'" (Oct. 8, 1980). As we're gradually loosed from the chains of lust, we're freed to love according to God's original plan. This is "a living morality," the Pope says, in which we realize the very meaning of our humanity (see April 16, 1980).

Freedom from the Law

Most people look at Christian morality—especially sexual morality—as an oppressive list of rules to follow. How far this misunderstanding is from the "living morality" proclaimed by Christ! The Gospel doesn't give us more rules to follow. The Gospel is meant to *change our hearts* so that we no longer need the rules (see CCC, n. 1968). To the degree that we experience this change of heart, we experience "freedom from the law" (see Rom 7; Gal 5)—not freedom to break the law; freedom to *fulfill* it.

Here's an example of what freedom from the law looks like: Do you have any desire to murder your best friend? This may seem like an odd question, but it actually demonstrates the point. Assuming you do not, then you don't need the commandment "Thou shalt not murder thy best friend" because you have no desire to break it. To this extent you are "free from the law." In other words, you don't experience this law ("Thou shalt not murder thy best friend") as an imposition because your heart already conforms to it.

Before sin, the human heart conformed totally to God's will. For example, the first married couple didn't need a law forbidding adultery. They had no desire to commit adultery (and not only because there was no one else around). Only with "flat-tire syndrome" do we experience a rupture between our desires and God's will for us. Here's where the law serves its essential purpose. It's given to convict us of sin (see Rom 7:7). However, when Christ says "You have heard the commandment ... but I tell you ..." he indicates that we need something more than mere precepts can offer.

The Old Testament law is good and just, but it "does not of itself give the strength, the grace of the Spirit, to fulfill it" (CCC, n. 1963). In other words, it convicts us of "driving with flat tires" but it doesn't re-inflate those tires. "The Law of the Gospel," however, "proceeds to reform the heart, the root of human acts, where man chooses between the pure and the impure" (CCC, n. 1968).

To the degree that we allow Christ to "re-inflate our tires," we no longer need the law because we no longer desire to break it. What laws do you still need? What teachings of the Church feel like a burden or imposition to you? Perhaps the problem isn't with the law or with the Church, but with your own "hardness of heart." Don't throw away the law; surrender your disordered desires to Christ and let him transform them.

Trying to follow all the rules without seeking air for our flat tires is futile. Those who do will either become self-righteous hypocrites or they'll abandon God's law for a rationalized, watered-down version of the Gospel. Either way it's a "gospel" without the good news; it's Christianity without Christ. Both the self-righteous and the lawless have yet to "pass-over" from the bondage of the ethical code to the freedom of the "new ethos"—the freedom of redemption.

Such freedom liberates us not from the *external* "constraint" that calls us to good, but from the *internal* constraint that hinders our choice of the good. When we *desire* what is true, good, and beautiful, then we are free indeed—free to love, free to bless, which is the freedom from the compulsion to *grasp* and *possess*. Those who toss off the law in order to indulge their lusts may imagine themselves free, but like an alcoholic who can't say no to the bottle, a person who can't say no to lust is *enslaved*. "For freedom Christ has set us free; stand fast therefore, and do not submit again to a yoke of slavery" (Gal 5:1).

The Grace of Creation Becomes the Grace of Redemption

As John Paul says, living in this freedom "is a still uncertain and fragile journey as long as we are on earth, but it is one made possible by grace, which enables us to possess the full freedom of the children of God (see Rom 8:21)" (VS, n. 18). We are not justified by the law; no one can keep it. We are "justified by ... grace as a gift, through the redemption which is in Christ" (Rom 3:24).

What is *grace?* John Paul describes it as God's mysterious gift to the human heart that enables men and women to live in the mutual and sincere gift of self (see Jan. 30, 1980). In the beginning, man and woman were infused with grace. When they doubted God's love and "denied the gift," they fell from grace. If this is the source of the problem, what's the first step toward a solution? Faith. If original sin is our denial of God's gift, "*faith,* in its deepest essence, is *the openness* of the human heart to the gift: *to God's self-communication in the Holy Spirit*" (DV, n. 51).

The Pope observes that when Christ calls us to overcome lust in the Sermon on the Mount, his words bear witness that the original grace of creation has become for each of us the grace of redemption (see Oct. 29, 1980). The Son of God took on flesh and died on a cross so that our sinful humanity might be put to death. He rose from the dead to "re-create" our humanity. He ascended bodily into the life of the Trinity to "in-spire" our bodies once again with God's life and love. Through this gift of our redemption, Christ breathes back into our flesh that same Spirit (grace) that "ex-pired" from our bodies when we denied the gift (see Jn 20:22).

Repent and Believe in the Good News

Jesus' whole life bears witness to the truth we find so hard to believe: God loves us; he is unequivocally *for* us, not against us. The "banquet" really exists and everyone without exception is invited. The only "requirement" for entry is that we stop eating out of the dumpster.

In essence, Christ's life proclaims: "You don't believe God loves you? Let me show you how much God loves you. You don't believe that God is 'gift'? This is my body *given* for you (see Lk 22:19). You think God wants to keep you from life? I will bleed myself dry so that my life's blood can give you life to the full (see Jn 10:10). You thought God was a tyrant, a slave-driver? I will take the form of a slave (see Phil 2:7); I will let you 'lord it over' me to demonstrate that God has no desire to 'lord it over' you (see Mt 20:28). You thought God would whip your back if you gave him the chance? I will let you whip my back to demonstrate that God has no desire to whip yours. I have not come to condemn you, but to save you (see Jn 3:17). I have not come to enslave you, but to set you free (see Gal 5:1). Stop persisting in your unbelief. Repent and believe in the good news" (see Mk 1:15).

As we open ourselves to this gift, the grace of redemption begins to "re-vivify" our humanity, to enliven our hearts with God's own goodness. To the degree that we allow this grace to inform and *transform* us, God's Holy Spirit impregnates our sexual desires "with everything that is noble and beautiful," with "the supreme value which is love" (Oct. 29, 1980).

Where is the grace of redemption poured out? Primarily in the sacramental life of the Church. Sacraments aren't merely religious rituals. They "inject sanctity into the plan of man's humanity: they penetrate the soul and body, [our] femininity and masculinity ... with the power of sanctity" (July 4, 1984). In other words, sacraments make Christ's death and resurrection a *living reality* in our own lives. Unfortunately many Christians fail to "tap into" the power of the sacraments. Through baptism alone, it's as if we've been given a trillion dollars in our bank accounts, but few of us seem to withdraw more than about seventy-five cents. In the sacraments, God's love is "poured into our hearts through the Holy Spirit" (Rom 5:5). We need to "bank" on this gift.

Life in the Spirit and the Redemption of the Body

In St. Paul's terminology, living the life of grace is synonymous with living "according to the Spirit." He contrasts this with "living according to the flesh." Walk "by the Spirit, and do not gratify the desires of the flesh. For the desires of the flesh are against the Spirit, and the desires of the Spirit are against the flesh" (Gal 5:16-17).

This does *not* mean, as many a Christian has tragically concluded, that St. Paul condemns the body or thinks of it as an inherent obstacle to living a "spiritual" life. As we have already learned in our study of the Pope's teaching, the body is the specific vehicle of the spiritual life. In this context, "the flesh" refers to the whole person (body and soul) cut off from God's "in-spiration," cut off from God's indwelling Spirit. It refers to a person dominated by lust and the other vices. In turn, the person who lives "according to the Spirit" does *not* reject his body, but opens his whole body-soul personality to divine "inspiration."

With great hope, John Paul II proclaims that as much as lust enslaves us by disordering our passions, so much does this "life according to the Spirit" free us to be a gift to others. As much as lust blinds us to the truth of God's plan for the body, so much does "life according to the Spirit" open our eyes to the body's nuptial meaning (see Dec. 1, 1982). So, to the degree that we open ourselves to "life in the Spirit" we also experience the "redemption of our bodies" (Rom 8:23).

John Paul II insists that "the redemption of the body" isn't only a heavenly reality. We await its fulfillment then, but it is already at work in us now. This means as we allow our lusts to be "crucified with Christ" (see Gal 5:24) we can progressively rediscover in what is erotic that original "nuptial meaning of the body" and live it. John Paul II says that this "liberation from lust" and the freedom it affords is, in fact, the condition for living all of life together in truth (see Oct. 8, 1980).

Purity Is Not Prudishness

To the degree that we live the redemption of our bodies, we understand that sexual purity isn't a matter of "annihilating" or repressing sexual attraction and desire. As Karol Wojtyla, the future Pope John Paul II, wrote in *Love & Responsibility*, mature purity "consists in quickness to affirm the value of the person in every situation, and in raising [sexual reactions] to the personal level" (LR, 170-171). In the Sermon on the Mount, Christ is not simply saying "don't look." John Paul explains that Jesus' words are "an invitation to a pure way of looking at others, capable of respecting the spousal [or nuptial] meaning of the body" (VS, n. 15).

Obviously, if a person needs to turn away in order to avoid lusting, then, by all means, "don't look." For the person who is bound by lust, the Old Testament admonition, "Turn away your eyes from a shapely woman" (Sir 9:8) retains all its wisdom. We classically call this "avoiding the occasion of sin" by "gaining custody of the eyes." This is a necessary first step, but the Pope would describe such an approach as a "negative" purity. As we grow in virtue we come to experience "positive" or "mature" purity. "In mature purity man enjoys the fruits of the victory won over lust." He enjoys the "efficacy of the gift of the Holy Spirit" who restores to his experience of the body "all its simplicity, its explicitness, and also its interior joy" (April 1, 1981).

Practically everyone begins the journey towards mature purity on the "negative" side. Unfortunately, many people stagnate at this stage thinking it's all they can expect. Keep going! Needless to say, I'm far from being a perfect man, but I can attest to the fact that as we appropriate the gift of redemption in our lives, lust loses sway in our hearts. We come not only to understand, but to *see* and *experience* the body as a "theology," a sign of God's own mystery. "Blessed are the pure in heart, for they shall see God" (Mt 5:8). If we understand what the Pope is holding out to us here, we can add: "Blessed are the pure in heart, for they shall see God's mystery revealed through the body."

Purity, therefore, is not prudishness. It does *not* reject the body. "Purity is the glory of the human body before God. It is God's glory in the human body, through which masculinity and femininity are manifested" (March 18, 1981). Purity in its fullness will only be restored in heaven. Yet, as the *Catechism* teaches, "Even now [purity of heart] enables us to see *according to* God ... it lets us perceive the human body—ours and our neighbor's—as a temple of the Holy Spirit, a manifestation of divine beauty" (CCC, n. 2519).

We have to reckon with the fact that we have a Pope who, in the restoration project of the Sistine Chapel, ordered the removal of several loincloths that previous popes had painted over Michelangelo's original nudes. And he did this in the name of Christian purity. During the homily dedicating the restored frescos, John Paul proclaimed the Sistine Chapel "*the sanctuary of the theology of the human body.*" He added, "It seems that Michelangelo, in his own way, allowed himself to be guided by the evocative words of the Book of Genesis which ... reveals: 'The man and his wife were both naked, yet felt no shame' (Gn 2:25)." (April 13, 1994).

What, then, is the difference between pornography and a proper artistic portrayal of nakedness? The Pope says the difference lies in the intention of the artist. Pornographic portrayals of the body raise objection "not because of their object, since the human body in itself always has its inalienable dignity—but because of the quality or way of its reproduction" (May 6, 1981). The pornographer seeks only to arouse lust in the viewer, while the true artist (such as Michelangelo) helps us see "the whole personal mystery of man." Proper portrayals of the naked body teach us "in a way that nuptial meaning of the body which corresponds to, and is the measure of, 'purity of heart'" (May 6, 1981). Those who experience mature purity understand the naked body for what it is—the revelation of God's plan of love.

The Interpretation of Suspicion

Doubters respond, "Impossible! The naked body will always arouse lust." For the person dominated by lust, this is true. But, applying one of the Pope's boldest declarations of redemption, "of which man are we speaking? Of man *dominated* by lust or of man *redeemed by Christ?* This is what is at stake: the *reality* of Christ's redemption. *Christ has redeemed us!* This means he has given us the possibility of realizing the *entire truth* of our being; he has set our freedom free from the *domination* of lust" (VS, n. 103).

As Karol Wojtyla wrote in *Love & Responsibility,* we cannot simply equate nakedness with immodesty and lust. Immodesty is certainly present "when nakedness plays a negative role with regard to the value of the person, when its aim is to arouse [lust]." But, Wojtyla adds, "this is not inevitable" (LR, 190-191). If we think a "lustful look" is the only way a person *can* look at the human body, then we subscribe to what John Paul II calls "the interpretation of suspicion." Those who live by suspicion remain so locked in their own lusts that they project the same bondage on to everyone else. They can't imagine any way to think about the human body and the sexual relationship other than through the prism of lust.

When we hold the human heart "in a state of continual and irreversible suspicion" (Oct. 29, 1980) because of lust, we condemn ourselves to a hopeless, loveless existence. We condemn ourselves to following the rules (ethics) without a change of heart (ethos). Eventually we abandon God's law because we simply cannot keep it. This kind of permanent suspicion effectively cuts us off from the *power* of the Gospel.

As St. Paul warns us, we must avoid the trap of "holding the form of religion" while "denying the power of it" (2 Tm 3:5). "Redemption is a truth, a reality, in the name of which man must feel called, and called with efficacy" (Oct. 29, 1980). In other words, the death and resurrection of Christ is *effective.* It can change our lives, our attitudes, our hearts—yes—our sexual desires. *"Do not empty the cross of its power!*" (see 1 Cor 1:17). John Paul exclaims that this "is the cry of the new evangelization" (OL, n. 3).

Much is at stake. "The meaning of life is the antithesis of the interpretation 'of suspicion.' This interpretation is very different, it is radically different from what we discover in Christ's words in the Sermon on the Mount. These words reveal ... another vision of man's possibilities" (Oct. 29, 1980). Unless we tap into this "other vision of man's possibilities," we will find it impossible to love as Christ loves; we will remain cut off from the meaning of life.

Growing in Mature Purity

So how do we tap into this "other vision of man's possibilities"? How do we progress from "negative" purity to "positive"? I'll begin with a quote from the Pope and then add some personal reflections.

To grow in purity, the Pope says we "must be committed to a progressive education in self control of the will, of the feelings, of the emotions; and this education must develop beginning with the most simple acts in which it is relatively easy to put the interior decision into practice" (Oct. 24, 1984). For example, what are your eating habits? If you can't say no to a potato chip, how are you going to say no to indulging in lust? Fasting is a wonderful way to grow in mastery of our passions. If this isn't already part of your life, start with a simple sacrifice that's relatively easy to put into practice. As you continue exercising this "muscle," you will find your strength increasing. What was once "impossible" gradually becomes possible.

The muscle analogy, however, is only half right. Growing in purity certainly demands human effort, but we're also aided by supernatural grace. Here it's crucial to distinguish between indulgence, repression, and redemption. When lust "flares up," most people think they only have two choices: indulge or repress. If these are the only options, which one looks more "holy"? Repression. Perhaps this is why many Christians have serious sexual problems. Yet there is another way! Rather than repress lust by pushing it into the subconscious, trying to ignore it, or otherwise seeking to annihilate it, we must *surrender* our lusts to Christ and allow him to slay them. As we do, "the Spirit of the Lord gives new form to our desires" (CCC, n. 2764). In other words, as we allow lust to be "crucified," we also come to experience the "resurrection" of God's original plan for sexual desire. Not immediately, but gradually, progressively, as we take up our cross every day and follow, we come to experience sexual desire as the power to love in God's image.

This process of transformation requires not only a resolute will but also a firm faith. It's the Holy Spirit who transforms our hearts, who "re-inflates our tires." And faith, you may recall, is the openness of the human heart to God's gift of the Holy Spirit (see DV, n. 51).

When lust tempts you, or even overwhelms you, you might say a prayer like this: *Lord, I thank you for the gift of my sexual desires. I surrender this lustful desire to you and I ask you please, by the power of your death and resurrection, to "untwist" in me what sin has twisted so that I might experience sexual desire as you intend—as the desire to love in your image.*

To reinforce your decision to "die" to lust, you may also want to place yourself in the shape of a cross—hands outstretched—while repeating the above prayer. The point here is to conform yourself to Christ, to carry "in the body the death of Jesus, so that the life of Jesus may also be manifested in your bodies" (2 Cor 4:10).

Resolving *not* to indulge lust can be very difficult, at times even emotionally and physically wrenching. It seems few men and women experience the freedom for which

Christ has set us free because when they taste this kind of "crucifixion," rather than staying the course which leads to resurrection, they "come down from the cross." When those nails are biting into your hands, and the burden of the cross seems too heavy to bear, keep going! You are on the verge of a passover from death to life, from lust to authentic love. Only if we are willing to die with Christ can we also live the resurrected life he offers.

Discerning the Movements of Our Hearts

Let me emphasize—if this isn't clear enough already—that the "positive" approach to purity I'm outlining with the Pope's help does not provide a license to "push the envelope." The person who uses anything in this book as an excuse to indulge his (or her) lusts isn't seeking purity. Honest people know their limits. They know what situations would make them stumble and avoid them with the seriousness Christ demands of us. "If your right eye causes you to sin, pluck it out ... if your right hand causes you to sin, cut it off" (Mt 5:29-30). Modern adaptation: "If your computer causes you to sin, throw it away. If your TV causes you to sin, get rid of it."

It is true that sometimes love and lust are difficult to distinguish. A man, for example, upon recognizing a woman's beauty, might wonder where the line is between seeing her as an object for his own gratification and loving her rightly as a person made in God's image. As John Paul writes, lust "is not always plain and obvious; sometimes it is concealed, so that it passes itself off as 'love.'... Does this mean that it is our duty to distrust the human heart? No!" the Pope insists. "It only means that we must keep it under control" (July 23, 1980).

"Control" here doesn't mean merely dominating unruly desires in order to keep them "in check." Again, that's only the "negative" side of the picture. As we mature in self-control, we experience it as "the ability to direct [sexual] reactions, both as to their content and their character" (Oct. 31, 1984). The person who is truly master of himself is able to direct erotic desire "towards the true, good, and beautiful—so that what is 'erotic' also becomes true, good, and beautiful" (Nov. 12, 1980). As this happens we come to understand and experience the mystery of sexuality "in a depth, simplicity, and beauty hitherto altogether unknown" (July 4, 1984).

To paraphrase a very insightful passage, the Pope points out that getting to this point demands "perseverance and consistency" in learning the meaning of our bodies, the meaning of our sexuality. We must learn this not only in the abstract (although this, too, is necessary), but above all in the interior reactions of our own "hearts." This is a "science," the Pope says, which can't really be learned only from books, because it's a question here of deep knowledge of our interior life. Deep in the heart we learn to distinguish between what, on the one hand, composes the great riches of sexuality and sexual attraction, and what, on the other hand, bears only the sign of lust. And although these internal movements of the heart can sometimes be confused with one another, we have been called by Christ to acquire a mature and complete evaluation. And the Pope concludes, "It should be added that this task *can* be carried out and is really worthy of man" (Nov. 12, 1980).

Let's close this chapter with a prayer for purity.

Lord, help me to discern the movements of my heart. Help me to distinguish between the great riches of sexuality as you created it to be and the distortions of lust. I grant you permission, Lord, to slay my lusts. Take them. Crucify them so that I might come to experience the resurrection of sexual desire as you intend. Grant me a pure heart. Amen.

Chapter 4

BEYOND THE FIG LEAVES:
THE RESURRECTION OF THE BODY

Those who respond to the wedding invitation "will rejoice one day
with the beloved, in a happiness and rapture that can never end."
—CCC, n. 1821

We've looked briefly at our origin before sin and
our history affected by sin yet redeemed in Christ.
Now, in order to have a total vision of what it means to
be human, we must look to our ultimate destiny when
(assuming we say "yes" to the divine plan) God will raise
our bodies in glory.

Returning to our image of the deflated tires, our
destiny cannot be understood only as a return to the fully
"inflated" state of the beginning. In the resurrection
we enter into an entirely *new* dimension of human life
"beyond all understanding and description" (CCC, n.
1027). Tires, you might say, will give way to *flight*.

Heaven – A Bodily Experience

Many people have an erroneous "super-spiritual"
view of heaven. Such people tend to see the body
as a shell that they're anxious to get rid of. This is
not the Christian view of things. Christians conclude
their Creed with the bold proclamation: "I believe
in the resurrection of the body and life everlasting.
Amen." The *Catechism* observes, "'On no point does

the Christian faith meet with more opposition than on the resurrection of the body.' It is very commonly accepted that the life of the human person continues in a spiritual fashion after death. But how can we believe that this body, so clearly mortal, could rise to everlasting life" (CCC, n. 996)? What a mystery! In Christ "the mortal puts on immortality" (1 Cor 15:54).

We often speak of the "souls" in heaven. When we buried my grandmother, I saw her body go in the ground and I'm confident that her soul is now enjoying some form of union with God. But the souls currently in heaven ("currently," of course, is a time-bound word that doesn't even apply to heaven) remain in an "inhuman" state until the resurrection of their bodies. It can't be any other way for us as human beings. Since God created us as a union of body and soul, the separation of the two at death is entirely "unnatural." Our bodies will certainly be different in their resurrected state (recall that the disciples didn't readily recognize Jesus after the resurrection [see Lk 24:15-16]), but we will still have them!

The difference is that our bodies will be perfectly "spiritualized" (see 1 Cor 15:44). Spiritualization means that "the forces of the spirit will permeate the energies of the body" (Dec. 9, 1981). And because the "spirit" that will permeate our bodies is not only our own human, created spirits, but the divine, uncreated Holy Spirit, John Paul II speaks also of the "divinization" (making divine) of the body. In a way totally inaccessible to us now, we will participate, body and soul, "in the divine nature" (2 Pt 1:4).

Recall our earlier discussion of God's innermost secret: "God himself is an eternal exchange of love, Father, Son, and Holy Spirit, and he has destined us to share in that exchange" (CCC, n. 221). This is what we mean by the "spiritualization" and "divinization" of the body. To the degree that creatures can, we will share—body and soul—in God's eternal exchange of love. And this "great mystery" is prefigured right from the beginning in man and woman's "exchange of love," that is, in and through their "one flesh."

So, many ask, will there be sex in heaven? It depends what we mean by the term. Sex is not first what people *do*. It's who people *are* as male or female. John Paul II mentions three times in his audience of December 2, 1981 (and on other occasions throughout this cycle) that we will be raised *as male and female*. So, in this sense, yes, there will be sex in heaven. But, as we'll learn from Christ's words about the resurrection, the union of the sexes as we know it now will give way to an *infinitely greater* union. Those who are raised in glory will experience a bliss so far superior to earthly sexual union that our wee brains can't even begin to imagine it. Eye has not seen, ear has not heard, nor has it even dawned on us what God has prepared for those who love him (see 1 Cor 2:9).

Christ Points Us to the Ultimate "Marriage"

In his discussion with the Pharisees, Christ called men and women of history to look to "the beginning" in order to understand God's original plan for the sexual relationship. In his discussion with the Sadducees, Christ points us to an entirely new dimension of human sexuality and our call to union when he says that "in the resurrection they neither marry nor are given in marriage" (Mt 22:30). These words form the basis of John Paul II's reflections on the destiny of man and woman.

At first glance, Christ's words may seem to undermine all we've said about the greatness of marital love and the sexual embrace. But examined more closely, these words point to the crowning glory of all we've said. Marriage and the "one flesh" union exist from the beginning to point us to the "marriage of the Lamb" (Rv 19:7), to the union of Christ and the Church (see Eph 5:31-32). In the resurrection, the "primordial sacrament" will give way to the divine reality. In other words, if God created the union of the sexes as a foreshadowing of heaven, Christ is saying, "You no longer need a foreshadowing to point you *to* heaven when you're *in* heaven. You're there. The ultimate union has come."

People often ask, "Does this mean I won't be with my spouse in heaven?" Assuming you both say "yes" to God's wedding invitation, you will certainly be together. All who respond will live "together" in a communion that fulfills superabundantly all that is good, true, and beautiful about marriage and family life here on earth. What we need to understand is that the union of the sexes, as beautiful and wonderful as it is, is not our be-all and end-all. It's only an "icon," a sign of something infinitely greater. Paraphrasing the Holy Father, marriage doesn't express definitively the deepest meaning of sexuality. It merely provides a concrete expression of that meaning within history (see Jan. 13, 1982). At the end of history, the "historical" expression of sexuality will make way for an entirely new expression of our call to life-giving communion.

Icons and Idols

When we lose sight of that infinitely greater union, we inevitably treat the icon as an idol. In other words, when we lose sight of the joys of heaven we tend to view sexual union and its physical pleasures as our ultimate fulfillment. Welcome to the world in which we live.

Still, there's an important element of truth in our society's idolatrous obsession with sex. Behind every false god we discover our desire for the true God gone awry. The sexual confusion so prevalent in our world and in our own hearts is simply the human desire for heaven gone berserk. Untwist the distortions and we discover the astounding glory of sex in the divine plan. "For this reason ... the two become one flesh." For what reason? To reveal, proclaim, and anticipate the eternal union of Christ and the Church (see Eph 5:31-32).

God gave us sexual desire, you might say, as the fuel of a rocket that's meant to launch us into the stars and beyond. Yet, what would happen if the engines of that rocket became inverted, pointing us back only upon ourselves and no longer toward the stars? Launch that rocket and the result is a massive blast of self-destruction. Herein we discover the importance of Christ's words about the new state of the body and sex in the resurrection: They help us set our sights on the union that alone can satisfy. When we let the "power" of these words sink into our hearts, they redirect our rocket engines toward the stars. The idol once again becomes the icon it was meant to be.

Only when our engines are pointed toward the stars does marriage take on its true meaning as a sacrament. Sacraments, when properly lived, give us a taste of heaven on earth. But when heaven comes, the sacraments, having served their purpose, give way. There will be no sacraments in heaven (see CCC, n. 671), not because sacraments are annihilated, but because they're superabundantly fulfilled. Hence, the fact that we no longer marry in the resurrection shouldn't cause sadness, but rejoicing. Every human longing, every desire of the heart for love and union will be fulfilled beyond our wildest dreams. That deep "ache" of solitude will finally be completely and eternally satisfied.

Experience attests that even the most wonderful marriage doesn't fully satisfy our hunger for love and union. We still yearn for "something more." I love my wife, Wendy, more than any words can express, but she won't mind my saying that she is not my ultimate fulfillment. Do not hang your hat on a hook that cannot bear the weight! If we look to another human person as our ultimate fulfillment, we will crush that person. Only the eternal, ecstatic, "marriage" of heaven—so far superior to anything proper to earthly life that we can't begin to fathom it—can satisfy the human "ache" of solitude.

The Beatific Vision

There are clear and important distinctions between our original, historical, and ultimate existence. But there is also a continuity. In short, if our origin and our history revolve around the "great mystery" of divine love and nuptial communion, then our heavenly existence will revolve around the same, albeit in an entirely new dimension. Now we see dimly, as in a mirror, but then we will behold the Mystery "face to face" (see 1 Cor 13:12).

"Because of his transcendence, God cannot be seen as he is, unless he himself opens up his mystery to man's immediate contemplation and gives him the capacity for it. The Church calls this contemplation of God in his heavenly glory 'the beatific vision'" (CCC, n. 1028). "Beatify" means to make supremely happy. The unsurpassed beauty and splendor of the eternal vision of God will fill all who behold with never-ending bliss.

Recall man and woman's original "face to face" vision of each other. This provides a faint glimmer or prefiguration of the beatific vision. As John Paul says, man and woman experienced a "beatifying immunity from shame" in their nakedness precisely because their vision was infused with love. "Happiness is being rooted in love," the Pope affirms (Jan. 30, 1980). Man and woman had no fear of being fully "seen" by the other because each loved and received the other in the full truth of his or her naked humanity. Their mutual vision expressed their profound, personal "knowledge" of each other. They "participated" in the sheer goodness of each other's humanity.

John Paul writes that the beatific vision of heaven is "a concentration of knowledge and love on God himself." This knowledge "cannot be other than full participation in the interior life of God, that is, in the very trinitarian reality" (Dec. 16, 1981). In the beatific vision we will *know* God and he will *know* us (he already does, of course). We will *participate* "fully" in God's divinity and he will *participate* fully in our humanity (he already does, of course, having taken on human nature in the Incarnation).

God has humbled himself to share in our humanity so that we might share in his divinity. What a glorious exchange! As the *Catechism* says, The "Son of God became man so that we might become God" (CCC, n. 460), so that we might participate in the divine nature (see 2 Pt 1:4). This, of course, does not mean that we will lose our human nature and become on par with God. It does mean, though, that God will give us a share in his own divinity, to the degree that our humanity will allow.

This divine-human exchange expresses something of the "content" or inner dynamic of the beatific vision. Recall here that this is exactly what the serpent convinced us God was withholding—his divine life and our happiness. "If you want to be 'like God,'" he insinuated "you need to *grasp* it." No! God has always desired for us to share fully in his own divinity. It is a free gift. All we need do is open to *receive* it. We need not grasp at what God freely gives us. Sin—and all human misery—begins right here, with grasping at the gift.

Fulfillment of the Nuptial Meaning of the Body

How will this glorious exchange between God and man take place? Since the "nuptials" of heaven are beyond all human knowledge, all we can do is speculate. Yet, once again, we see a faint glimmer of what's to come in the nuptials of earth.

The original exchange of man and woman took place through the "freedom of the gift" and the "nuptial meaning of the body." Recall that God gave us freedom as the capacity to love, as the capacity to make a "sincere gift" of ourselves to one another. "Man can only find himself through the sincere gift of self" (GS, n. 24). Furthermore, God inscribed this call to self-donation right in our bodies as male and female. Our bodies have a "nuptial meaning" because they're capable of expressing divine love, "that love precisely in which the person becomes a gift and—by means of this gift—fulfills the very meaning of his being and existence" (Jan. 16, 1980).

Paraphrasing John Paul II, in the resurrection we discover—in a new, eternal dimension—the same nuptial meaning of the body. This time, however, the nuptial meaning of the body is fulfilled in our meeting with the mystery of the living God, through our vision of him "face to face" (see Dec. 9, 1981). The Pope does not elaborate, but applying the spousal analogy, we can conclude that in the resurrection, the divine Bridegroom will express his gift ("this is my body given for you") in its fullest reality. All who respond to the wedding invitation will open to receive this gift as Christ's bride. In response to this gift, we will give ourselves totally to the divine Bridegroom in an eternally life-giving embrace.

As the *Catechism* states, the Church "longs to be united with Christ, her Bridegroom, in the glory of heaven" where she "will rejoice one day with [her] Beloved, in a happiness and rapture that can never end" (CCC, n. 1821). John Paul writes that in this heavenly reality "penetration and permeation of what is essentially human by what is essentially divine, will then reach its peak" (Dec. 9, 1981).

The nuptial imagery is unmistakable. Of course, when using nuptial union as an image of heaven, it's more important than ever to remember the inadequacy of analogies. Caution is necessary. Heaven is not some eternally magnified experience of sexual union on earth. As John Paul II observes, the union to come "will be a completely new experience." Yet "at the same time," he says, "it will not be alienated in any way" from the love that man and woman experienced in "the beginning" and have sought to reclaim throughout history (see Jan. 13, 1982). The original meaning of the body "will then be revealed again in such simplicity and splendor" when all who respond to the wedding invitation will live in the full freedom of self-giving love (see Jan. 13, 1982). Those who rise to eternal life will experience "the absolute and eternal nuptial meaning of the glorified body in union with God himself" (March 24, 1982).

The Communion of Saints

We will live this self-giving love not only as individuals in union with God. As alluded to earlier, we will also live in self-giving love and communion with all the saints who enjoy the beatific vision. Recall that, in his experience of solitude, Adam discovered his fundamental vocation: love of God *and* love of neighbor. Heaven fulfills both dimensions of this vocation. When we reach our ultimate destiny we will live in consummate union with all who are raised in glory.

"*For man*, this consummation will be the final realization of the unity of the human race, which God willed from creation. ... Those who are united with Christ will form the community of the redeemed, 'the holy city' of God, 'the Bride, the wife of the Lamb'" (CCC, n. 1045). What was "the unity of the human race which God willed from creation"? It was the unity of the two, male and female, in "one body" (Gn 2:24). In the communion of saints there are "many parts" (a great multitude of glorified men and women), yet all are united eternally in "one body" (see 1 Cor 12:20).

This obviously will not be experienced in the sexual sense lived here on earth. Yet, we can conclude that in some mysterious way beyond earthly comprehension, all that is masculine in our humanity will be in union with all that is feminine in our humanity. That unity—that "one body"—will be the one Bride of Christ living in consummate union with her Bridegroom for eternity. In and through this communion with Christ, the communion of saints will live in communion with *the* Communion, the Trinity. We will *see* all and *be seen* by all. We will *know* all and *be known* by all. And God will be "all in all" (Eph 1:23).

As if it needs to be said again, *this* is the purpose of sexual union in the divine plan: to prefigure in some way the glory, ecstasy, and bliss that awaits us in heaven (see Eph 5:31-32). As the *Catechism* expresses it, "In the joys of their love [God gives spouses] here on earth a foretaste of the wedding feast of the Lamb" (CCC, n. 1642).

No wonder we're all so darned interested in sex. God put an innate desire in every human being to want to understand it. Why? To lead us to him. But beware of the counterfeits! Because sex is meant to launch us toward heaven, the devil attacks right here. When our innate "curiosity" about sex is not met with the "great mystery" of the divine plan, we inevitably fall, in one way or another, for the counter-plan. In other words, when our desire to understand the body and sexuality isn't met with the truth, we inevitably fall for the lies.

Our God Is Rich in Mercy

If you have fed your curiosity about sex with lies, don't despair. Our God is rich in mercy. Why was Christ so compassionate toward sexual sinners, especially women? Because, behind their deception, he knew that they were looking for him, the true Bridegroom.

Think of the woman caught in adultery (see Jn 8: 2-11). She went looking for love, intimacy, union with another, but, as always, the counterfeit couldn't satisfy. Laden with shame, she was brought before Christ by an angry crowd anxious to stone her. Christ then said whoever was without sin could cast the first stone. According to his own words, the sinless Christ could have thrown a stone, but Christ came not to condemn. He came to save (see Jn 3:17).

St. John writes that "Jesus was left alone with the woman standing before him" (Jn 8:9). Reading into the story a bit, we can imagine that in the woman's encounter with the divine Bridegroom she had a conversion from the counterfeit to the real thing. Do you think when Jesus said, "Go, and do not sin again" (Jn 8: 11), that she turned and grumbled, "Who is this man to tell me what I can and cannot do with my body!"? Or do you think, having encountered the love she was truly looking for, she left transformed, renewed, affirmed in the deepest part of her being as a woman? This is what Christ offers to us all!

What are the lies you have believed? What are the counterfeits you have bought into? Behind them all is your authentic thirst for love. Sexual sin is a quest to satisfy that thirst with a tonic that never can. Christ meets us right there without condemnation. As he said to another sexual sinner in just such a meeting, "If you knew the gift of God ... you would have asked him and he would have given you living water" (Jn 4:10). Sin denies the gift. Faith opens to receive it and is satisfied.

Be not afraid! Throw your sexuality wide open to Christ. Christ *never* robs us of our humanity. He fully reveals it to us: "Christ, by the revelation of the mystery of the Father and his love, fully reveals man to himself and makes his supreme calling clear" (GS, n. 22). What is that "supreme calling"? Here's the theological answer: Our supreme calling is to be part of the communion of saints, who participate in communion with Christ in the Communion of the Trinity. Here's the translation: Our supreme calling is eternal ecstasy; unrivaled rapture; bounteous, beauteous bliss.

Lord, grant us faith. Help us believe in this glorious gift. Amen.

Chapter 5

CHRISTIAN CELIBACY: A MARRIAGE MADE IN HEAVEN

Celibacy for the kingdom signifies "the risen man, in whom there will be revealed ... the absolute and eternal nuptial meaning of the glorified body in union with God himself."
—John Paul II (March 24, 1982)

We looked briefly at our origin, history, and destiny in order to answer the question "What does it mean to be human?" We now shift gears to the second half of John Paul II's theology of the body in order to address the question "How am I supposed to live my life in a way that will bring true happiness?" In other words, returning to our favored image, once we've acquired some air in our tires, where should we drive the car? The Pope answers this question in terms of life vocation.

John Paul II writes: "Christian revelation recognizes two specific ways of realizing the vocation of the human person, in its entirety, to love: marriage and virginity or celibacy. Either one is in its own proper form an actuation of the most profound truth about man, of his being 'created in the image of God'" (FC, n. 11). In this cycle, John Paul looks at the celibate vocation. Once again, he begins with the words of Christ.

Eunuchs "For the Kingdom"

When Jesus restored the permanence of marriage according to God's original plan, his disciples (like many today) concluded that it was better not to marry at all (see Mt 19:10). In response to their contention, Jesus takes the discussion to a different plane altogether: "For there are eunuchs who have been so from birth, and there are eunuchs who have been made eunuchs by men, and there are eunuchs who have made themselves eunuchs for the sake of the kingdom of heaven" (Mt 19:12).

A eunuch is someone physically incapable of sexual relations. In the Christian tradition, a eunuch "for the kingdom of heaven" is someone who freely forgoes sexual relations in anticipation of that state in which men and women "neither marry nor are given in marriage." Celibacy for the kingdom, therefore, "is a sign that the body, whose end is not the grave, is directed to glorification." It "is a witness among men that anticipates the future resurrection" (March 24, 1982). In a sense, the celibate man or woman steps beyond the dimensions of history—while living within the dimensions of history—and proclaims to the world that "the kingdom of God is here"; the ultimate marriage has come.

Christian celibacy, therefore, is not a rejection of sexuality. It points us to the ultimate purpose and meaning of sexuality. "For this reason ... the two become one flesh." What reason does St. Paul give? Man and woman become one flesh as a sign or "sacrament" of Christ's eternal union with the Church (see Eph 5:31-32). Those who remain celibate for the kingdom "skip" the earthly sacrament of marriage in anticipation of the heavenly reality, the "marriage of the Lamb." If it is "not good for man to be alone," Christian celibacy reveals that the ultimate fulfillment of solitude is found only in union with God. In a way, the celibate person freely chooses to remain in the "ache" of solitude in this life in order to devote all of his longings to the union that alone can satisfy.

The word "celibacy," unfortunately, doesn't usually convey this deeper meaning. It's a negative word in the sense that it tells us what these people are *not* doing. "Eunuch" has even worse connotations. Perhaps we would do better to define this vocation in terms of what it embraces and anticipates versus what it gives up. It embraces and anticipates "the heavenly marriage."

Celibacy Must Be Freely Chosen

A survey recently circulated among priests posed a question something like this: "Should celibacy be a free choice or should it continue to be *imposed by the Church?*" Contrary to widespread opinion, the Church forces *no one* to be celibate. Christ's words ("there are eunuchs who have *made themselves* eunuchs") "clearly indicate the importance of the personal choice" of this vocation (March 10, 1982). If someone were *forced* into celibacy, it would be no more legitimate than if someone were *forced* into marriage.

We tend to forget in the Latin Church (*Roman* Catholicism) that male celibacy is a vocation in itself, apart from priesthood. The Catholic and Orthodox Churches of the East not only have a valid married priesthood, they also have a vibrant non-ordained celibate brotherhood. As the *Catechism* indicates, the Latin Church usually chooses her priests from among men of faith who have chosen celibacy as their life's vocation (see CCC, n. 1579). This seems to imply that the choice of celibacy should come first. If a Roman Catholic man has discerned a celibate vocation, then, within his life of celibacy, he might also discern a call to priesthood. Those priests who believe celibacy was foisted on them, it seems, haven't understood these important distinctions.

As a result, many today are clamoring for an end to priestly celibacy. Some even blame celibacy itself for the sexual problems and abuses of some of the clergy. As I wrote in my book *Good News About Sex & Marriage,* "Celibacy does not *cause* sexual disorder. Sin does. Simply getting married does not *cure* sexual disorder. Christ does. If a priest, or any other man, were to enter marriage with deep-seated sexual disorders, he would be condemning his wife to a life of sexual objectification. The only way the scandal of sexual sin (whether committed by priests or others) will end is if people experience the redemption of their sexuality in Christ" (p. 163).

Authentic Christian celibacy witnesses dramatically to this redemption. It is true that, as a *discipline* of the Latin Church (rather than a doctrine), the practice of reserving priestly ordination to those men who have chosen a celibate life could change. But when we realize how celibacy points us to the ultimate meaning of sex, we recognize that our world needs the witness of Christian celibacy now more than ever.

Celibacy Flows from the Redemption of Sexuality

To a world bound by lust, life-long celibacy seems absurd. The world's general attitude towards Christian celibacy might be summarized like this: "Hey, marriage is the only 'legitimate' chance you Christians get to indulge your lusts. Why the heck would you ever want to give that up? You'd be condemning yourself to a life of hopeless repression." But recall that indulgence and repression are not the only choices. There is another way unknown to the world (and sadly, unknown to many Christians as well). As we've already said, "Jesus came to restore creation to the purity of its origins" (CCC, n. 2336).

The difference between marriage and celibacy must *never* be understood as the difference between having a "legitimate" outlet for sexual lust on the one hand and having to repress it on the other. Christ calls *everyone*—no matter his or her particular vocation—to experience redemption from the domination of lust. Only from this perspective do the Christian vocations (celibacy *and* marriage) make any sense. *Both* vocations—if they are to be lived as Christ intends—flow from the same experience of the redemption of sexual desire.

John Paul states that the celibate person must submit "the sinfulness of his [fallen] nature to the forces that spring from the mystery of the redemption of the body ... just as any other man does" (April 7, 1982). This is why he indicates that the call to celibacy is not only a matter of formation but of *transformation* (see May 5, 1982). The person who lives this transformation is not bound to indulge his lusts. He is free with the freedom of the gift. For such a person, sacrificing sexual union (the icon) for the sake of the kingdom (the reality to which the icon points) not only becomes a possibility, it becomes quite attractive. The reality is infinitely more attractive than the icon! Those who think otherwise have turned the icon into an idol.

St. Paul's Teaching

In this context it's important to understand properly St. Paul's teaching about marriage and celibacy in 1 Corinthians, chapter 7. He writes that people who "cannot exercise self-control ... should marry. For it is better to marry than to be aflame with passion" (v. 9). Is marriage only intended for those who "can't handle" celibacy? Does marriage suddenly make a person's lack of self-control (lust) "okay"? Not according to John Paul II.

The Pope reminds us that we cannot interpret Paul's words apart from Christ's words about lust. The verb translated "to be aflame" signifies lust. "To marry" signifies the ethical order—the call to overcome lust— that St. Paul consciously introduces in this context (see Dec. 1, 1982). So, according to John Paul II, it seems that St. Paul is saying something like this: "It is better to overcome lust through the grace of marriage than to remain engulfed by its flames."

John Paul II acknowledges that St. Paul speaks of marriage and celibacy in 1 Corinthians, chapter 7 in a style "totally his own" (June 23, 1982) without sparing "entirely personal accents" (July 14, 1982). The Pope even asks if St. Paul's statements indicate a "personal aversion" to marriage. When taken out of context, verses such as "It is well for a man not to touch a woman" (v. 1); "I wish that all were [celibate] as I myself am" (v. 7); and "Do not seek marriage" (v. 27) might lead one to believe so. But the Pope demonstrates that a thoughtful reading of the whole text leads to a different conclusion.

St. Paul directly combats the badly mistaken idea circulating in Corinth that marriage and sexual union were sinful. Marriage is a "special gift from God" (v. 7). Spouses "should not refuse one another" in their sexual relationship "except perhaps by agreement" (v. 5). And St. Paul commends those who marry for "doing well" (see v. 38).

Is Celibacy "Better" Than Marriage?

Why, then, does St. Paul say that "he who refrains from marriage will do better" (v. 38)? Based on these words, the Church has traditionally taught that celibacy is an objectively "superior" vocation. But this must be understood with great care lest we fall into serious error.

Many have erroneously concluded that if celibacy is "so good," marriage must be "so bad." If refraining from sex makes one "pure and holy," having sex—even in marriage—must make one "tainted and dirty." This is *absolutely not* the mind of the Church! Such devaluations of marriage and sexual union actually stem from the Manichean heresy we spoke of in the first chapter.

John Paul II makes it perfectly clear: "The 'superiority' of [celibacy for the kingdom] to matrimony in the authentic Tradition of the Church never means disparagement of marriage or belittlement of its essential value. It does not ... mean a shift, even implicit, on the Manichean positions, or a support of ways of evaluating or acting based on the Manichean understanding of the body and sexuality." In the authentic teaching of the Church "we do not find any basis whatever for any disparagement of matrimony" (April 7, 1982).

Celibacy is the "exceptional" calling because marriage remains the "normal" calling in this life. It is "better" not because of celibacy itself, but because it's chosen *for the kingdom*. It is better in the sense that the heavenly marriage (to which celibates devote themselves more directly) is superior to the earthly marriage. Christian celibacy gives those who live it authentically an even more intense "foretaste" of the communion to come with God and with all the saints.

Does this mean if we *really* wanted to follow God we would all be celibates? No. As St. Paul writes, "Each has his own special gift from God, one of one kind and one of another" (v. 7). We must carefully and prayerfully discern which "gift" God has given us. Subjectively speaking, the "better" vocation is the one God calls us to as our own personal gift. If marriage is your gift, rejoice! This is your path to happiness. If celibacy is your gift, rejoice! This is your path to happiness.

Marriage and Celibacy Complement Each Other

Marriage and celibacy obviously differ in important ways. Yet these differences don't conflict. The values of one and the other vocation "interpenetrate each other." In fact, marriage and celibacy "explain and complete each other" (April 14, 1982). Marriage reveals the spousal nature of the celibate vocation just as the celibate vocation reveals the great value of marital union. Let me explain.

How does marital love shed light on the nature of the celibate vocation? John Paul II writes that the fidelity and "total self-donation" lived by spouses provide a model for the fidelity and self-donation required of those who choose the celibate vocation. Both vocations in their own way express marital or conjugal love, which entails "the total gift of oneself" (see April 14, 1982). Furthermore, the fruit of children in married life helps celibate men and women realize that they are called to a fruitfulness as well—a fruitfulness of the spirit. In these ways we see how the "natural" reality of marriage points us to the "supernatural" reality of celibacy for the kingdom. In fact, full knowledge and appreciation of God's plan for marriage and family life are indispensable for the celibate person. As the Pope expresses it, in order for the celibate person "to be fully aware of what he is choosing ... he must also be fully aware of what he is renouncing" (May 5, 1982).

Celibacy, in turn, "has a particular importance and special eloquence for those who live a married life" (April 14, 1982). Celibacy, as a direct anticipation of the marriage to come, shows couples what their union is a sacrament of. In other words, celibacy helps married couples realize that their love also is oriented toward "the kingdom." Furthermore, by abstaining from sexual union, celibates demonstrate the great value of sexual union. How so? A sacrifice only has value to the degree that the thing sacrificed has value. For example, we don't give up sin for Lent; we're supposed to give up sin *all the time*. If our sacrifice is to mean anything, we must sacrifice something of *real value*. The Church values celibacy so highly *precisely* because she values what it sacrifices—sexual union and all that is connected to it—so highly.

Once again, the self-denial involved in such a sacrifice must not be conceived as a repression of sexuality. Celibacy for the kingdom is meant to be a fruitful living out of the redemption of sexual desire, understood as the desire to make of oneself a "sincere gift" for others.

Celibacy Expresses the Nuptial Meaning of the Body

As we can see, marriage and celibacy are much more closely related than most people realize. Both vocations provide "a full answer" to the meaning of sexuality (see July 14, 1982). That meaning is "self-donation" in the image of God. As a result, it shouldn't surprise us that whenever a culture devalues sexuality, it inevitably devalues both marriage *and* the celibate vocation. The sexual revolution of the 20th century has certainly demonstrated this in practice.

The Pope insists that the celibate life Christ spoke of must flow from a "profound and mature knowledge of the nuptial meaning of the body." Only on this basis does celibacy for the kingdom "find full warranty and motivation" (April 28, 1982). Thus, if someone were to choose this vocation based on a fear or rejection of sex, or because of deep-seated sexual wounds that prevented a healthy married life, it would not correspond to Christ's invitation (see April 28, 1982).

No one can reject the nuptial meaning of his body without doing violence to his humanity as a man or woman made in God's image. The nuptial meaning of the body "is the fundamental element of human existence in the world" (Jan. 16, 1980). It reveals that the human person is created to be a gift "for" another. Christ's words about celibacy "consequently show that this 'for,' present from the beginning at the basis of marriage, can also be at the basis of continence 'for' the kingdom of heaven." Therefore, "on the basis of the same nuptial meaning of [the] body ... there can be formed the love that commits man to marriage for the whole duration of his life, but there can be formed also the love that commits man to a life of continence 'for the sake of the kingdom of heaven'" (April 28, 1982).

The point is that our sexuality calls us to give ourselves away in life-giving love. The celibate person doesn't reject this call. He just lives it in a different way. Every man, by virtue of the nuptial meaning of his body, is called in some way to be both a husband and a father. Every woman, by virtue of the nuptial meaning of her body, is called in some way to be both a wife and a mother. As an image of Christ, the celibate man "marries" the Church. Through his bodily gift of self he bears numerous "spiritual children." As an image of the Church, the celibate woman "marries" Christ. Through her bodily gift of self she bears numerous "spiritual children." This is why the terms husband, wife, father, mother, brother, and sister are applicable both to marriage and family life *and* priestly and religious life.

The Celibate Marriage of Joseph and Mary

We will conclude our discussion of celibacy by looking briefly at the "oddity" of Joseph and Mary's celibate marriage. The Catholic Church teaches that Mary and Joseph were given the exceptional calling to embrace both the celibate vocation and the marital vocation *at the same time.* In other words, they lived the earthly marriage and the heavenly "marriage" simultaneously. In turn, their celibate marriage literally affected the marriage of heaven and earth. For the fruit of their total, virginal gift of self was the Word made flesh—heaven come to earth (see March 24, 1982). In this way Joseph and Mary "became the first witnesses of a fruitfulness different from that of the flesh, that is, of a fruitfulness of the Spirit: 'That which is conceived in her is of the Holy Spirit' (Mt 1:20)" (March 24, 1982).

Joseph and Mary remained celibate not because "sex is bad." As a married couple, they were given the exceptional calling to live their sexuality according to its ultimate meaning—total self-donation to God. By embracing that "heavenly dimension" of sexuality on earth, they enabled heaven to penetrate earth. Recall that sexual union, from the beginning, was meant to foreshadow the union of God and man, Christ and the Church. Undoing Eve's "no," Mary, the new Eve, represents the whole human race in giving her "yes" to God's marriage proposal (see CCC, nn. 411, 505). In a sense, even in her journey on earth, Mary was already participating in the "nuptials" of heaven. For her to engage in the nuptial embrace of earth would have been a "step backward," so to speak.

If the Church holds out the Holy Family as a model for all families, this does not imply that married couples who want to be "really holy" should never have sex. If such were the case, "holy" families would eventually mean no families due to their failure to procreate. Joseph and Mary are a model for all married couples because of their example of total self-donation. The normal call is for spouses to model the Holy Family by living their "one flesh" union in total self-donation. In this way, spouses also "bring Christ to the world" because the marital embrace—when lived as God intends—proclaims the mystery of Christ (see Eph 5:31-32).

We will unfold the way in which the "one flesh" union proclaims the mystery of Christ more precisely in the next chapter.

Chapter 6

CHRISTIAN MARRIAGE: IMAGING CHRIST'S UNION WITH THE CHURCH

"Authentic married love is caught up into divine love."
—GS, n. 48

We continue to seek an answer to the question "How am I supposed to live my life in a way that brings true happiness?" The quick answer is to love as God loves, in "sincere self-giving." Celibacy for the kingdom is one way to do this. But it's clearly the exception to the rule. Marriage and family life remain the normal vocation. However, as John Paul II observes, if "anyone chooses marriage, he must choose it just as it was instituted by the Creator 'in the beginning'" (April 21, 1982). If married life is based on anything other than God's original plan, it is sure to disappoint; it is sure to lead to heartache rather than happiness.

How, then, can couples reclaim God's original plan? The *Catechism* responds: "By coming to restore the original order of creation disturbed by sin, [Christ] himself gives the strength and grace to live marriage in the new dimension of the Reign of God." Therefore, "by following Christ, renouncing themselves, and taking up their crosses ... spouses will be able to 'receive' the original meaning of marriage and live it with the help of Christ" (CCC, n. 1615). As we will see more clearly in this chapter, marriage, when lived authentically, plunges spouses right into the heart of the mystery of Christ.

A "Summa" of Christian Teaching

St. Paul's famous (or, in our day, infamous) passage from Ephesians 5 serves as the basis for the Pope's reflections on the sacrament of marriage. One verse in particular causes the hair on the back of women's necks to stand up—"Wives, be subject [or submit] to your husbands." Oh boy, here we go....

It's true that some men throughout history have used this verse to justify their own sinful domination of women. (Yes, according to Genesis 3:16, male domination is the direct result of *sin*.) But, before you dismiss St. Paul as a male chauvinist, wait until you discover John Paul II's winning interpretation of his words. The Pope resurrects the true meaning of Ephesians 5 by applying one of the most important rules of biblical interpretation: read each verse *in context*. Here's the entire passage:

> Be subject to one another out of reverence for Christ. Wives, be subject to your husbands, as to the Lord. For the husband is the head of the wife as Christ is the head of the Church, his body, and is himself its Savior. As the Church is subject to Christ, so let wives also be subject in everything to their husbands. Husbands, love your wives, as Christ loved the Church and gave himself up for her, that he might sanctify her, having cleansed her by the washing of water with the word, that he might present the Church to himself in splendor, without spot or wrinkle or any such thing, that she might be holy and without blemish. Even so husbands should love their wives as their own bodies. He who loves his wife loves himself. For no man ever hates his own flesh, but nourishes and

> cherishes it, as Christ does the Church, because we
> are members of his body. "For this reason a man
> shall leave his father and mother and be joined
> to his wife, and the two shall become one flesh."
> This is a great mystery, and I mean in reference to
> Christ and the Church (Eph 5:21-32).

Reaching beyond the polemics we must try "to understand possibly 'to the very depths' how much richness of the truth revealed by God is contained in the scope of [this] wonderful page" (July 28, 1982). This "key and classic text," as the Pope describes it, immerses us in the glory and greatness of God's plan for creating us male and female and calling us to sexual union. Even more, it serves as "the compendium or *summa*, in some sense, *of the teaching about God and man* which was brought to fulfillment by Christ" (LF, n. 19).

If God's spousal love for humanity was only "half-open" in the Old Testament, here the mystery is "fully revealed (but of course without ceasing to be a mystery)" (Sept. 22, 1982). In turn, through this revelation of God's spousal love, we become "witnesses of a particular meeting of [God's] mystery with the very essence of the vocation to marriage" (Aug. 11, 1982).

St. Paul's Evangelical Genius

Like all of us, St. Paul was certainly affected by his culture. As the Pope writes, he "does not fear to accept those concepts which were characteristic of the mentality and of the customs of the times. ... Nowadays our contemporary sensitivity is certainly different; quite different, too [is] the social position of women in regard to men" (Aug. 11, 1982). But if we simply dismiss St. Paul's words as nothing but a product of his "politically incorrect" culture, we miss his evangelical genius altogether. Like any great evangelist, St. Paul appeals to the language and customs of the culture he's trying to reach, while injecting that language and those customs with the mystery of Christ.

In Ephesians 4 (remember *context* is key), St. Paul states explicitly that Christians "must no longer live as the Gentiles do." They "are darkened in their understanding ... due to their hardness of heart." So put off "your old nature which ... is corrupt through deceitful lusts ... and be renewed in the spirit of your minds, and put on the new nature, created after the likeness of God in true righteousness and holiness" (Eph 4:17-18, 22-24). This should all sound very familiar to us by now. Who also spoke of "hardness of heart" and how it distorts the sexual relationship? Who also invited men and women to live in "true righteousness and holiness" by experiencing redemption from lust? Like Christ, St. Paul is calling men and women *back to God's original plan*! He's calling men and women to live according to the divine image in which God originally made them.

When the contested (and detested) verses of Ephesians 5 are read in their full context, we realize that—far from demeaning women and absolving abusive men—St. Paul is restoring the only sure foundation for the proper balance of love between the sexes. In effect, we might conclude that St. Paul is saying something like this: "Sure, since this is the language you're used to, we can talk about 'submission' in marriage. But that means one thing to the Gentiles. Here's how it must look for followers of Christ."

Mutual Subjection and Reverence for Christ

Notice that the first thing St. Paul says to spouses is "Be subject [or submit] to *one another* out of reverence for

Christ" (v. 21). As John Paul II emphasizes, Ephesians 5 calls spouses to a *mutual* subjection. Those who think St. Paul was simply regurgitating cultural prejudice against women do not understand how counter-cultural this idea was.

The Pope insists that when St. Paul writes "be subject to your husbands" (v. 22), he "does not intend to say that ... marriage is a pact of domination of the husband over the wife. ... Love makes the husband simultaneously subject to the wife" (Aug. 11, 1982). He adds that being "subject" to one's spouse means being "completely given" (Aug. 18, 1982). Therefore mutual subjection means "a reciprocal donation of self" (Aug. 11, 1982). It means both spouses realize and live the nuptial meaning of their bodies, which calls them to mutual and sincere self-giving.

Christ, who "gave up his body" for his Bride, must be the source and the model of this self-giving. Christian spouses give themselves up for one another "out of reverence for Christ" (v. 21). John Paul II goes so far as to say that this reverence "is none other than a spiritually mature form" of the mutual attraction of the sexes (July 4, 1984). In other words, "reverence for Christ" results from a lived experience of the redemption of sexual attraction and desire. Through ongoing conversion we gradually come to experience that mature level of purity we spoke of previously.

Pure men and women *see* the mystery of Christ revealed through their bodies. It's not just a religious concept; pure men and women *feel* it in their hearts. They realize that the call to union inscribed in their sexuality is a "great mystery" that proclaims the union of Christ and the Church. When we experience this as the "content" of our sexual attractions, we don't want to lust—we want to genuflect. When we live as St. Paul calls us to, lust is *unthinkable.* The "great mystery" of sexuality fills us instead with profound amazement, awe, and wonder. In other words, it fills us with *reverence for Christ.*

The Virtuous Husband

As a practical example of husbands living a redeemed sexuality in subjection to their wives, I often point to this eye-opening passage from the Pope's book *Love & Responsibility.* It not only shows that Karol Wojtyla (the Pope's pre-papal name) was and is no prude, but, more importantly, it calls men to self-control and tenderness out of deep respect and reverence for their wives. Wojtyla wrote that if a husband is truly to love his wife, "it is necessary to insist that intercourse must not serve merely as a means of allowing [his] climax. ... The man must take [the] difference between male and female reactions into account ... so that climax may be reached [by] both ... and as far as possible occur in both simultaneously." The husband must do this "not for hedonistic, but for altruistic reasons." In this case, if "we take into account the shorter and more violent curve of arousal in the man, [such] tenderness on his part in the context of marital intercourse acquires the significance of an act of virtue" (LR, pp. 272, 275).

Please read this passage to anyone and everyone who thinks the Pope or the Church is "down on sex." How far from the truth! As an astonished engaged woman once exclaimed when I read this passage, *"The Pope rocks!"*

History attests that few men express the tenderness and virtue the Pope speaks of in the passage above. As a whole, women have suffered greatly at the hands of male lust and domination, just as Genesis predicted (see Gn 3:16). So, to all the women reading this book, if you have never heard this, it's long overdue. Allow me, as a representative of the male side of the human race, to apologize humbly for the way male lust has wounded you. The wounds go so very deep in a woman's soul, and I am so very, very sorry. Please forgive us. We know not what we do.

To the men I say, get ready. Are you up to the mission St. Paul assigns us? I'm going to call you forth into battle—a battle that involves all the courage and stamina you can muster; a battle that involves death, bloodshed, and much sacrifice. If there are warped men who are willing *to kill* in order to indulge their lusts (behind virtually every abortion is a man of lust), we, instead, must be men who are willing *to die* rather than ever indulge our lusts.

Submission within the Spousal Analogy

In a world void of such heroic, sacrificial men, the feminist revolt against Ephesians 5 is quite understandable. In the absence of redemption, St. Paul's words can only be viewed as an admonition for wives to resign themselves to male lust and tyranny. But redemption has been accomplished! The knowledge that Christ died and rose again to empower us to live according to God's original plan of love deeply imbues St. Paul's entire teaching on marriage. He presents redemption itself through the analogy of spousal love and sexual union.

According to the analogy, the wife images the Church and the husband images Christ. The analogy obviously breaks down (e.g., no husband perfectly images Christ), yet it speaks volumes not only about Christ's "spousal" love for us, but also about the very essence and meaning of marriage. We learn that marriage "corresponds to the vocation of Christians only when it reflects the love which Christ the Bridegroom gives to the Church, his Bride, and which the Church ... attempts to return to Christ" (Aug. 18, 1982). Apart from this model, marriage can sink quite quickly into a form of oppression, especially for women.

Again, St. Paul uses the language of his day but injects it with an entirely new, redemptive meaning. When we understand the nature of the analogy he's using, it makes sense for him to say, "Wives be subject [or submit] to your husbands as to the Lord" (v. 22). One way I explain "submission" in this context is, "Wives, put yourself *under* (sub) the *mission* of your husband." What's the mission of the husband? Here it is gentlemen: "Husbands, love your wives *as Christ loved the Church*." How did Christ love the Church? He "gave himself up for her" (v. 25)—unto death! Christ said that he came not to be served *but to serve*, and to lay down his life for his Bride (see Mt 20:28).

"Headship" Is a Call to Serve

Why are we so quick to accuse St. Paul of justifying male domination? Based on what we've unfolded, when St. Paul writes, "Wives, submit to your husbands" he's saying, "Wives, allow your husbands to *serve you*." To which I respond, "Who's got it worse here?" We've got the whole thing flipped upside down! Not that the wife is the master and the husband a slave. Power, control, domination—these are the wrong paradigms altogether, regardless of "who's the boss." Christian marriage calls spouses to a *mutual service*, or, as St. Paul says, a mutual "subjection." Yet, according to the nature of sexual difference, each lives this service in different, complementary ways.

If Ephesians says that "the husband is the head of the wife as Christ is the head of the Church," this means the husband must be *the first to serve* (see Lk 22:25-26). There is a "sacred order" to love. In imaging Christ and the Church, John Paul II writes that "the husband is above all *he who loves*, and the wife, on the other hand is *she who is loved*." Thus, we can conclude with the Pope that "the wife's 'submission' to her husband, understood in the context of the entire passage ... signifies above all 'the experiencing of love.' All the more so since this 'submission' is related to the image of the submission of the Church to Christ, which certainly consists in experiencing his love" (Sept. 1, 1982).

Is this demeaning towards women? Imagine what marriage would be like if husbands took St. Paul's words to heart. Imagine if husbands throughout the world preferred to die rather than ever violate the dignity of their wives. Isn't this the example Christ gave us? And isn't this the kind of love women are looking for? Isn't this what the knight-in-shining-armor romantic fantasy is all about?

Restoration of Holiness

Spouses who commit themselves to St. Paul's vision of marriage—properly understood—find that the grace of their sacrament (in conjunction with the other sacraments) gradually re-inflates their "tires." In other words, they experience their love for each other as something beautifully healing and redemptive. Marital love not only participates in the mystery of creation through pro-creation, it also participates in the mystery of redemption. As the Pope says, authentic marital love "is redeeming love, love as salvation" (Aug. 18, 1982).

Even here on earth, the grace of Christ's spousal love begins restoring in us something of the holiness experienced by the first married couple. "Christ loved the Church and gave himself up for her ... that she might be holy" (vv. 25-27). But, as we all know, holiness is not something automatic. In all our trials and struggles, we must continually open ourselves like a bride to receive the gift of Christ's love, allowing it to *in*form and *trans*form us. As John Paul II writes, "Holiness is measured according to the 'great mystery' in which the Bride responds with the gift of love to the gift of the Bridegroom" (MD, n. 27).

Holiness, then, is not first a matter of *doing*, but of *letting it be done to us* (see Lk 1:38). We must allow Christ to "crucify" all our disordered ways of relating. We must allow him to sanctify us (make us holy) "by the washing of water with the word" (v. 26). Scripture scholars see in this a reference to baptism. It was customary in St. Paul's day for the bride to precede her wedding with a cleansing bath in preparation for her bridegroom. The *Catechism* describes baptism as "the nuptial bath which precedes the wedding feast, the Eucharist" (CCC, n. 1617). St. Paul also alludes to the nuptial gift of the Eucharist when he speaks of the "nourishment" Christ offers his Bride (see v. 29).

But marriage not only sheds light on baptism and the Eucharist. John Paul II observes that marriage serves as the model or *prototype* in some sense of all the sacraments of the new covenant (see Oct. 20, 1982). All the sacraments have a "nuptial" character since their purpose is to unite the Bride (the Church) with her Bridegroom (Christ). Through this grand analogy, the union of spouses becomes perhaps the most insightful way of understanding Christianity itself. "The entire Christian life bears the mark of the spousal love of Christ and the Church" (CCC, n. 1617).

Chosen in Christ from the Beginning

Just as God organically inscribed the marital union of Adam and Eve in the mystery of creation, he organically inscribes the "marital" union of the new Adam and the new Eve (Christ and the Church) in the mystery of redemption. Spousal union, in fact, becomes the foundation upon which God constructs the entire mystery of our salvation in Christ (see Sept. 29 and Oct. 13, 1982).

Here, in the "nuptial" character of both creation and redemption, we recognize an essential continuity regarding God's plan for humanity. We tend to think of Christ's coming as "plan B," necessitated when man and woman's sin supposedly thwarted "plan A." Our need of redemption from sin certainly flows from the reality of our fall. Yet God's plan for us to share in his own eternal "exchange of love" remains the same yesterday, today, and forever. Sin, you might say, caused a detour in the fulfillment of that plan, but it didn't thwart it. God's plan for man continues despite sin. That plan—forever and for always—is that all things would be taken up and united in Christ (see Eph 1:10).

John Paul II cannot stress enough that Christ—the Incarnate Christ—has always been at the center of God's plan for man and for the universe. As he wrote in the first line of his first encyclical letter, "Jesus Christ is the center of the universe and of history" (RH, n. 1). God destined us for union with Christ not only after sin and not only to redeem us from sin. God "chose us in [Christ] before the foundation of the world" (Eph 1:4).

This means that the grace of original innocence (recall the experiences of original solitude, unity, and nakedness) "was granted in consideration of him [Christ] ... even though—according to the dimensions of time and history—it had preceded the Incarnation" (Oct. 6, 1982). In other words, the love (grace) man and woman knew "in the beginning" through their bodies was a foretaste or preview in some sense of the love (grace) that Christ would pour out within history through his body. In fact, the love the first couple knew in their bodies *depended* in some sense on the love that Christ would pour out on his Bride, the Church. Creation foreshadows and prepares us for redemption; the union of the first Adam and Eve foreshadows and prepares us for the union of the new Adam and Eve, Christ and the Church.

Again, although it often demands a rethinking of commonly held perceptions, the Incarnation is not an afterthought in God's mind. As the *Catechism* confirms, "From the beginning, God envisaged the glory of the new creation in Christ" (CCC, n. 280). We can conclude this because St. Paul links the "one flesh" union of Genesis with the union of Christ and the Church. "'For this reason a man shall leave his father and mother and be joined to his wife, and the two shall become one flesh.' This is a great mystery, and I mean in reference to Christ and the church" (Eph 5:31-32). Right from the beginning—before sin—conjugal union foreshadowed the Incarnation, Christ's union with humanity in "one flesh."

This Is a "Great Mystery"

St. Paul's linking of the "one flesh" union with the union of Christ and the Church "is the most important point of the whole text, in a certain sense, the keystone" (Sept. 8, 1982). Both "the union of Christ with the Church, and the conjugal union of man and woman in marriage are in this way illuminated by a particular supernatural light" (Aug. 25, 1982).

Guided by this supernatural light, St. Paul demonstrates a keen understanding of the "sacramentality" of the body. Recall the broader sense of this term. The body is a "sacrament" in the sense that it makes visible the invisible. In examining Ephesians 5 the Pope recalls his thesis: "The body in fact, and only it, is capable of making visible what is invisible: the spiritual and divine. It was created to transfer into the visible reality of the world the mystery hidden from eternity in God, and thus to be its sign" (Oct. 6, 1982).

Recall what we mean by "the mystery hidden from eternity in God": (1) *God is a Communion of love* and (2) we are *destined to share in that exchange* through our union with Christ. John Paul writes that the "sacrament consists in the 'manifesting' of that mystery in a sign which serves not only to proclaim the mystery, but also to accomplish it in man" (Sept. 8, 1982). Sacramental signs truly bring about what they signify. St. Paul speaks of two signs—one from the order of creation and the other from the order of redemption—that truly communicate God's mystery of love.

In creation, the Pope says that God's mystery of love "became a *visible reality through the union* of the first man and woman" (see Gn 2:24). In redemption, that same mystery of divine love becomes *"a visible reality [through] the indissoluble union of Christ with the Church,* which the author of the letter to the Ephesians presents as the nuptial union of spouses" (Oct. 13, 1982). With regard to these signs, these two unions, "we are speaking ... in reference to the entire work of creation and redemption" (Oct. 13, 1982). This is the magnanimous capacity of sacramental signs. They mysteriously "contain" ultimate reality and put us in touch with it. They "embrace the universe," as John Paul II says.

The Meaning of Human Life

John Paul II remarks that it is of "special merit" to St. Paul that he "brought these two signs together [the "one flesh" union and the union of Christ and the Church], and made of them one great sign—that is, a great sacrament" (Sept. 29, 1982). Through this "great sacrament" the "great mystery" of human life is revealed.

The Pope observes that the linking of these two unions is obviously important "to the Christian vocation of husbands and wives." However, it "is equally essential and valid for understanding man in general: for the fundamental problem of understanding him and for the self-comprehension of his being in the world." Indeed, it is in this link that we "find the answer to the question concerning the meaning of 'being a body'" (Dec. 15, 1982).

What is that meaning? We are called to love as Christ loves. This is the new commandment Christ gives us, "Love one another as I have loved you" (Jn 15:12). How did Christ love us? "This is my body ... *given for you*" (Lk 22:19).

Remember the story of my father-in-law, the tears he shed when he received the Eucharist for the first time after consummating his marriage? My father-in-law realized that day that the meaning of life, the meaning of the universe, is inscribed not only in our souls, but in our bodies: in the "great mystery" of sexual difference and our call to become "one flesh."

The Language of the Body

According to John Paul II, divine love (agape) is the body's native "language." Yes, the body "speaks." It's meant to proclaim the love of Christ and the Church. It does so, as the Pope candidly expresses, by "means of gestures and reactions, by means of the whole dynamism ... of tension and enjoyment—whose direct source is the body in its masculinity and its femininity, the body in its action and interaction—by means of all this ... the person 'speaks.' ... Precisely on the level of this 'language of the body' ... man and woman reciprocally express themselves in the fullest and most profound way possible to them" (Aug. 22, 1984).

If "carnal love"—bodily, sexual love—is meant to express "the language of 'agape'" (Sept. 1, 1982), we must properly understand this language. Christ's love seems distinguishable by four particular qualities. First, Christ gives his body *freely* ("No one takes my life from me, I lay it down of my own accord," Jn 10:18). Second, he gives his body *totally*—without reservation, condition, or selfish calculation ("He loved them to the last," Jn 13:1). Third, he gives his body *faithfully* ("I am with you always," Mt 28:20). And fourth, he gives his body *fruitfully* ("I came that they may have life," Jn 10:10). If men and women are to avoid the pitfalls of counterfeit love, and live their vocation to its full, their union must express the same *free, total, faithful, fruitful* love that Christ expresses.

Another name for this kind of love is marriage. This is precisely what a bride and groom commit to at the altar. The priest or deacon asks them: "Have you come here *freely* and *without reservation* to give yourselves to each other in marriage? Do you promise to be *faithful* until death? Do you promise to *receive children* lovingly from God?" The bride and groom each say "yes."

In turn, spouses are meant to express this same "yes" *with their bodies* whenever they become one flesh. "Indeed the very words 'I take you to be my wife—my husband,'" the Pope says, "can be fulfilled only by means of conjugal intercourse." With conjugal intercourse "we pass to the reality which corresponds to these words" (Jan. 5, 1983). Intercourse, then, is where the words of the wedding vows *become flesh*. It's where men and women are meant to *incarnate* divine love. It's a fine thing when a couple returns to the Church to renew their vows on a special anniversary, but this shouldn't undermine the fact that every time a husband and wife have intercourse they're meant to renew their wedding vows with the "language of their bodies."

Distinguishing True and False Prophets

The Church's sexual ethic begins to make sense when viewed through this lens. The Church's teaching is not a prudish list of prohibitions. It's a call to embrace our own "greatness," our own God-given dignity. It's a call to live the love we're created for, the love we so ardently desire.

John Paul II goes so far as to describe the body and sexual union as "prophetic." A prophet is someone who speaks for God, who proclaims his mystery. But, as the Pope adds, we must be careful to distinguish between true and false prophets (see Jan. 26, 1983). If we can speak the truth with our bodies, we can also speak lies.

We all know it's possible to lie with our bodies. Suppose a used-car salesman knowingly sells you a lemon and then shakes your hand. Didn't he just lie with his body? What about the kiss of Judas? It was a lie. And who do you think prompts us to lie with our bodies? Could it be ... *Satan!*? *Saturday Night Live* "Church Lady" humor aside, the "father of lies" wants us to speak his own language with our bodies. Why? To keep us from the "great mystery" of Christ's union with the Church— that is, to keep us from eternal life.

Ultimately all questions of sexual morality come down to one very simple question: Does this act truly image God's *free, total, faithful, fruitful* love or does it not? If it does not, it is a counterfeit love that can never satisfy. In practical terms, how healthy would a marriage be if spouses were regularly unfaithful to their wedding vows? On the other hand, how healthy would a marriage be if spouses regularly renewed their vows, expressing an ever-increasing commitment to them? As we'll see more clearly in the next chapter, this is precisely what's at stake in the Church's teaching on sexual morality.

Chapter 7

THEOLOGY IN THE BEDROOM: A LIBERATING SEXUAL MORALITY

"Every man and every woman fully realizes himself or herself through the sincere gift of self. For spouses, the moment of conjugal union constitutes a very particular expression of this."
—John Paul II (LF, n. 12)

In this brief introduction to John Paul II's theology of the body, we've examined our origin, our history, and our destiny, and the vocations of celibacy and marriage. Now we have the proper context in which to understand the Church's teaching on sexual morality and procreation.

Perhaps at this point you're feeling some trepidation. You've understood the Pope's logic, you can see where it's headed, and you know your life doesn't "measure up." Welcome to the human race. We all fall short of the glory (see Rom 3:23). But the good news is that Christ can restore us to glory. Remember—it doesn't matter where you've been or what mistakes you've made. The theology of the body is a message of sexual salvation, not condemnation.

Authentic Christian morality is not against us. It is unstintingly *for* us. The first line in the *Catechism*'s section on morality speaks volumes. It is *not*, "Give up everything you really want and follow all these miserable rules or you're going to hell." It is "Christian, recognize your dignity ..." (CCC, n.

1691). This is what John Paul II's theology of the body has been proclaiming all along—our dignity, our "greatness" as male and female. Now it is time to see it through. Be not afraid!

Applying the Basic Principle

At the close of the last chapter, I observed that all questions of sexual morality ultimately come down to one question: Does this given act truly image God's *free, total, faithful, fruitful* love or does it not? My book *Good News About Sex & Marriage* uses this principle to answer 115 of the most common questions and objections to Church teaching. I refer you to that for a more detailed discussion. For now we'll just apply the principle to a few questions with the aim of arriving at the core of sexual morality.

If it challenges you, my challenge to you is to *let* it challenge you. We needn't fear the demands of love. We need only fear that "hardness of heart" Christ spoke of that resists the demands of love (see Mt 19:8). As you read the following questions, consider all we have learned about the "great mystery" of our creation as male and female and the call of the two to become "one flesh." Here we go.

Does masturbation image God's *free, total, faithful, fruitful* love or does it not? Does fornication (pre-marital sex) image God's *free, total, faithful, fruitful* love or does it not? Does adultery? Does homosexual behavior? Does viewing pornography? And here's where the rubber hits the road (pun intended): Does an intentionally sterilized act of intercourse between spouses image God's *free, total, faithful, fruitful* love or does it not? If today you hear his voice, harden not your hearts (see Heb 3:15).

Wise men and women throughout history (not only Catholics) have recognized that respect for the procreative function of sexual union is the linchpin of all sexual morality. Even Sigmund Freud recognized this. He wrote that the "abandonment of the reproductive function is the common feature of all perversions. We actually describe a sexual activity as perverse if it has given up the aim of reproduction and pursues the attainment of pleasure as an aim independent of it" (*Introductory Lectures in Psychoanalysis*).

Consider this: When we divorce sex from its natural orientation toward new life, what is left to prevent the justification of any and every means to sexual climax? When we sterilize sex we fundamentally disorient the act. It no longer points of necessity to marriage and the raising of a family. Indulging libido for its own sake becomes the name of the game and we eventually treat natural, vaginal intercourse as only one of a-million-and-one ways of indulging libido. When we pry sex loose from its most natural consequence, we inevitably lose our moral compass. Welcome to the world in which we live.

Sex and Marriage Redefined

The monogamous, life-long union of the sexes and the family that results have served as the bedrock of Western civilization for centuries. Yet during the 20th century—in only a few generations—sex, marriage, and the family have been radically deconstructed and redefined. Behaviors once commonly considered as an affront to human dignity and a serious threat to the social order are not only touted as goods to be pursued by the media, but are sanctioned and protected as legal "rights" by the government.

Have you ever wondered what brought about so radical a shift so quickly? The answer is complex, but one thing is certain: If the modern brand of sexual "liberation" was to flourish, the natural consequence of sex (procreation) *had* to be eliminated. The sexual revolution of the 20th century is simply inexplicable apart from the nearly universal acceptance of contraception.

Proponents of contraception in the early 1900's knew that advancing their cause would be impossible without the "blessing" of the Christian churches. Until 1930, Catholics, Orthodox, and Protestants stood together in their condemnation of any attempt to sterilize the marital act. That year, the Anglican Church broke with more than 1,900 years of uninterrupted Christian teaching. When the Pill debuted in the early 1960's, the Catholic Church was the only Christian body retaining what in thirty short years had come to be seen as an archaic, even absurd position.

Inspired by a widespread but faulty view of the Second Vatican Council, many expected that a papal blessing of contraception was imminent. Withstanding unimaginable global pressure, Pope Paul VI shocked the world when he reaffirmed the traditional teaching against contraception in his 1968 encyclical letter *Humanae Vitae* (*Of Human Life*). It fell like a bomb. The widespread dissent that immediately followed has not ceased to this day.

We Need a "Total Vision of Man"

Was Paul VI hopelessly "out of touch" with reality? Or, maybe—just maybe—was he speaking a difficult, yet unchangeable truth to a world blinded by its excesses? If you have resisted the Church's teaching on contraception, believe me, I can relate. In fact, I almost left the Catholic Church because of this "blasted teaching." "Gimme a break," I thought. "Denying people contraception is like denying people toothpaste or toilet paper. It's just another modern convenience. I should be able to express my love for my wife whenever I want without having to worry about raising fifteen kids!"

Pope Paul knew it would be difficult for the modern world to understand the immorality of contraception. Modern men and women have lost sight of the greatness, dignity, and divine purpose *of human life* (*Humanae Vitae*). When that happens, we no longer see the sexual union as a "great mystery" proclaiming God's love for humanity and foreshadowing heaven. We quickly reduce sex to a biological process subject to all sorts of human manipulations. Today, because of this mind-set, most men and women give no more thought to tinkering with their fertility than they do to tinkering with their hair color.

Sex is certainly biological, but that's only a partial perspective. As Paul VI observed, in order to understand Christian teaching on sex and procreation, we must look "beyond partial perspectives" to a "total vision of man and of his vocation" (HV, n. 7). This is what John Paul II set out to do in his theology of the body—provide the "total vision of man" that would enable us to understand the Church's teaching on contraception. In fact, John Paul II says that the entire theology of the body can be considered "an ample commentary on the doctrine contained in the encyclical *Humanae Vitae*" (Nov. 28, 1984).

All five of the preceding cycles have led us to this point. If I have successfully introduced you to John Paul II's beautiful vision of the body and sex, the basic logic of *Humanae Vitae* should be fairly clear. But important questions raised by Paul VI's encyclical still remain. What particular insight does John Paul II's theology of the body offer us in understanding *Humanae Vitae?* Why does the Church reject contraception but accept natural methods of regulating fertility? What does the Church mean by the practice of "responsible parenthood"? Doesn't the Church's teaching against contraception impede couples from expressing their love for one another?

Before we address these questions directly, we'll take a brief look at some key verses from the Song of Songs and the book of Tobit. John Paul II reflects on these as a sort of preface to his discussion of *Humanae Vitae.* Hence, they must contain elements that shed a helpful light on the above questions.

The Bride as "Sister" and "Enclosed Garden"

In that grand biblical ode to erotic love, the Song of Songs, the lover repeatedly refers to his beloved as "sister" *before* calling her "bride." "You have ravished my heart, my sister, my bride, you have ravished my heart with one glance of your eyes ... How sweet is your love, my sister, my bride! ... A garden locked is my sister, my bride, a garden enclosed, a fountain sealed" (Sng 4: 9-10,12). John Paul II sees "special eloquence" in this poetic expression.

Recognizing his beloved first as "sister" demonstrates that the lover respects her as a person who shares the same humanity. It echoes Adam's words, "This at last is bone of my bones and flesh of my flesh" (Gn 2:23). In short, seeing her first as "sister" demonstrates that his desire for her as "bride" is not one of lust but of love. The normal man recoils at the idea of lusting after his sister—and so should a man recoil at the thought of lusting after his bride. With "a disinterested tenderness" (May 30, 1984), the lover desires only to be a sincere gift to his beloved according to the image of God.

The groom demonstrates the genuine character of his love all the more with the expressions "garden enclosed" and "fountain sealed." These indicate that he upholds her as "master of her own mystery" (May 30, 1984). Every human person is an inviolable mystery as a unique reflection of God's own mystery. If the lover is to enter this "garden" and participate in the woman's mystery, he cannot barge in or break down the door. Nor can he manipulate her into surrendering the key. This would be rape. If he is to respect woman as "master of her own mystery," all the lover can do is entrust himself to her freedom. He puts "his hand to the latch" (Song 5:4) only with her freely given "yes." In total freedom—without any hint of coercion—she says: "I am my beloved's" (Song 6:3).

The point is that authentic love affords a certain "entering" into the mystery of the other person *without ever violating the mystery of the person* (see May 30, 1984). If a person's "love" violates the one loved, then *it is not love* and should not be called love. It is love's counterfeit—lust.

Sexual Union Is a Test of Life and Death

If the lovers in the Song of Songs help us distinguish between authentic love and lust, the marriage of Tobiah and Sarah in the Book of Tobit demonstrates just what's at stake in this distinction. We learn here that sexual union is "a test of life and death" (June 27, 1984).

As this Old Testament story goes, Sarah had already been married seven times, but each groom *died* before having intercourse with her (see Tb 6:13-14). (Talk about an anti-climactic honeymoon—and seven times in a row!) Then an angel appears to Tobiah and tells him that *he* is to marry Sarah. John Paul II—man of keen observation that he is—remarks that Tobiah had reason to be afraid. In fact, on the day of their wedding, Sarah's father was already digging Tobiah's grave! (see Tb 8:9)

Tobiah courageously faces the test. He takes Sarah as his wife, consummates the marriage—and lives. Why? Because "during the test on the wedding night, love, supported by prayer, is revealed as more stern than death." Love "is victorious because it prays" (June 27, 1984). Take a careful look at Tobiah's prayer. It contains a short review of everything we've discussed in the Pope's theology of the body.

> "Blessed art thou, O God ... and blessed be thy holy and glorious name for ever .... Thou madest Adam and gavest him Eve his wife as a helper and support. Thou didst say, 'It is not good that the man should be alone; let us make a helper for him like himself.' And now, O Lord, I am not taking this sister of mine because of lust, but with sincerity. Grant that I may find mercy and grow old together with her." And she said with him, "Amen" (Tb 8:5-8).

Tobiah first praises God for his sheer goodness. Then, as Christ will direct us to do, he sets his heart on God's original plan for marriage. He calls Sarah "sister" like the lover in the Song of Songs. He contrasts lust with the sincere gift of self. He knows that he needs God's mercy to live the truth of love, and he longs to spend his whole life with her. Sarah's "Amen" demonstrates that she shares one and the same desire.

If sexual union is a "test of life and death," then in the face of authentic nuptial love, death has no chance. "Where, O death, is your victory? Where, O death, is your sting?" (1 Cor 15:55). Spouses who by God's grace love one another according to God's original plan—and who trust in God's mercy when they fail to love one another rightly—have no fear of this "test." They are ready and willing to place themselves "between the forces of good and evil ... because love is confident in the victory of good and is ready to do everything so that good may conquer" (June 27, 1984).

Authentic marital love is ready to make any and every sacrifice so that lust does not trump love, so that the value *of human life* shines forth in all its beauty and splendor. This is the love to which the Church calls spouses in the encyclical *Humanae Vitae*. It is sacrificial love. It's the love with which "Christ loved the Church."

Ethics of the Sign

As the Pope writes, the teaching of *Humanae Vitae* "is closely connected with our previous reflections on *marriage in its dimension as a (sacramental) sign*" (July 11, 1984). We can argue against contraception entirely from human reason and philosophy. But John Paul II shows the deepest *theological* reason for the immorality of contraception—it is fundamentally sacrilegious because it falsifies the sacramental sign of married love.

As a sacrament, marriage not only symbolizes God's life and love, it *really participates* in God's life and love—or, at least, it is meant to. For sacraments to convey grace (God's life and love), the sacramental sign must accurately signify the spiritual mystery. For example, as a physical sign of cleansing, the waters of baptism bring about a true spiritual cleansing from sin. But if you were to baptize someone with mud or tar, no spiritual cleansing would take place because the physical symbol is now one of making dirty. This would actually be a counter-sign or an "anti-sacrament."

All of married life is a sacrament. All of married life is meant to be a sign of God's life and love. But this sacrament has a consummate expression. Nowhere do spouses signify God's love more profoundly than when they become "one flesh." Here, like no other moment in married life, spouses are called to participate in the "great mystery" of God's love. But this will only happen if their sexual union accurately signifies God's love. Therefore, as the Pope concludes, we "can speak of moral good and evil" in the sexual relationship "according to whether ... or not it has the character of the truthful sign" (Aug. 27, 1980).

John Paul II says that the essential element for marriage as a sacrament is the language of the body spoken in truth. This is how spouses "constitute" the sacramental sign of marriage (see Jan. 12, 1983). Insert contraception into the language of the body and (knowingly or unknowingly) the couple engages in a *counter-sign* of the "great mystery"—a kind of "anti-sacrament." Rather than proclaiming, "God is life-giving love," the language of contracepted intercourse says, "God is *not* life-giving love."

In this way spouses (knowingly or unknowingly) become "false prophets." They blaspheme. Their bodies still proclaim theology, but not Christian theology; not a theology of the God who reveals himself as Father, as Son, and as Holy Spirit. Contracepted sex denies and attacks our creation in the image of the Trinity.

Fidelity to the Wedding Vows

Most couples who use contraception simply have no idea that this is what they're saying with their bodies, so this is not a matter of assigning culpability. But even if a couple is innocent in this regard, contraception will still have its damaging effect on their relationship. For example, if I drink a cup of poison, but don't know it's poison, I haven't committed suicide and am not culpable for my own death. But it will still kill me. Whether I think it's poison or not has no bearing whatsoever on whether it is poison or not.

The causes of the dramatic rise in divorce in our culture are multiple and complex. Still, it shouldn't surprise us in the least that the spike in divorce has coincided with the acceptance and practice of contraception. What's the connection? In short, as I asked in the last chapter, how healthy would a marriage be if a husband and wife were regularly unfaithful to their wedding vows? Sexual intercourse is meant to renew and express wedding vows. But contraception turns the "I do" of those vows into an "I do not."

During conjugal intercourse, *"a moment so rich in significance*, it is ... especially important that the 'language of the body' be re-read in truth" (July 11, 1984). We are free to choose whether to engage in sex. But if we choose to engage in sex, we are not free to change its meaning. The language of the body has "clear-cut meanings," all of which are "programmed," the Pope says, in the conjugal consent, in the vows. For example, to "the question: 'Are you willing to accept responsibly and with love the children that God may give you ...' the man and the woman reply: 'Yes'" (Jan. 19, 1983).

If spouses say "yes" at the altar, but then render their union sterile, they are lying with their bodies. They're being unfaithful to their wedding vows. Such dishonesty at the heart of the marital covenant cannot *not* have a deleterious effect.

Someone might retort, "C'mon! I can commit to being 'open to children' at the altar, but this doesn't mean *each* and *every* act of intercourse needs to be open to children." But that makes as much sense as saying, "C'mon! I can commit to fidelity at the altar, but this doesn't mean *each* and *every* act of intercourse needs to be with my spouse." If you can recognize the inconsistency of a commitment to fidelity ... *but not always*, you should be able to recognize the inconsistency of a commitment to being open to children ... *but not always*.

Perhaps another way out of this logic is simply for a couple to exclude "openness to children" in the commitment they make at the altar. Then a couple wouldn't be "lying" with their bodies by using contraception, would they? It would reflect what they committed to, yes. But what they committed to would not be to love as God loves. What they committed to would not be marriage. Indeed, as the Church has always recognized, willfully excluding openness to children renders a marriage null from the start.

Responsible Parenthood

So, does fidelity to the wedding vows imply that couples are to leave the number of children they have entirely to "chance"? No. In calling couples to a responsible love, the Church calls them also to a responsible parenthood.

Pope Paul VI stated clearly that those are considered "to exercise responsible parenthood who prudently and generously decide to have a large family, or who, for serious reasons and with due respect to the moral law, choose to have no more children for the time being or even for an indeterminate period" (HV, n. 10). Notice that large families should result from prudent reflection, not "chance." Notice too that couples must have "serious reasons" to avoid pregnancy and must respect the moral law, the "ethics of the sign."

Assuming a couple has a serious reason to avoid a child (this could be financial, physical, psychological, etc.), what could they do that would not violate the consummate expression of their sacrament? In other words, what could they do to avoid conceiving a child that would not render them unfaithful to their wedding vows? You're doing it right now (I presume). They could *abstain* from sex. There is nothing wrong with abstaining from sex when there's a good reason to do so. The Church has always recognized that the *only* method of "birth control" that respects the language of divine love is "self-control."

A further question arises: Would a couple be doing anything to falsify their sexual union if they embraced during a time of natural infertility? Take, for example, a couple past childbearing years. They know their union will not result in a child. Are they violating "the sign" if they engage in intercourse with this knowledge? Are they contracepting? No. Contraception, by definition, is the choice to engage in an act of intercourse, but then do something else to *render* it sterile. This can be done by using various devices, hormones, surgical procedures, and the age-old method of withdrawal, or *coitus interruptus.*

Couples who use natural family planning (NFP) when they have a just reason to avoid pregnancy *never* render their sexual acts sterile; they never contracept. They track their fertility, abstain when they are fertile and, if they so desire, embrace when they are naturally infertile. Readers unfamiliar with modern NFP methods should note that they are 98-99%

effective at avoiding pregnancy when used properly. Furthermore, any woman, regardless of the regularity of her cycles, can use NFP successfully. This is not your grandmother's "rhythm method."

What's the Difference?

To some people this seems like splitting hairs. "What's the big difference," they ask, "between rendering the union sterile yourself and just waiting until it's naturally infertile? The end result is the same: both couples avoid children." To which I respond, what's the big difference between killing Grandma and just waiting until she dies naturally? End result's the same thing: dead Grandma. Yes, but one is a serious sin and the other is not. It is exactly the same with contraception and NFP.

As John Paul II observes, the difference between periodic abstinence (NFP) and contraception "is much wider and deeper than is usually thought, one which involves in the final analysis two irreconcilable concepts of the human person and of human sexuality" (FC, n. 32). The difference, in fact, is one of cosmic proportions.

First, it's important to realize that the Church has never said it is inherently wrong to avoid children. But the end (avoiding children) does not justify the means. There may well be a good reason for you to wish Grandma would pass on to the next life. Perhaps she is suffering terribly with age and disease. But this does not justify killing her. Similarly, you may have a good reason to avoid conceiving a child. Perhaps you are in serious financial straights. Perhaps you have four kids under the age of four and you have reached your emotional limits. But no scenario justifies rendering the sexual act sterile, just as no scenario justifies killing Grandma.

Grandma's natural death and a woman's natural period of infertility are both acts of God. But in killing Grandma or in rendering sex sterile, we take the powers of life *into our own hands*—just like the deceiver originally tempted us to do—and make ourselves like God (see Gn 3:5). Therefore, as the Pope concludes, "Contraception is to be judged so profoundly unlawful as never to be, for any reason, justified. To think or to say the contrary is equal to maintaining that in human life, situations may arise in which it is lawful not to recognize God as God" (Oct. 10, 1983).

Love or Lust?

One of the main objections to *Humanae Vitae* is that following its teaching (that is, practicing periodic abstinence when avoiding pregnancy) impedes couples from expressing their love for one another. But of what "love" are we speaking: authentic conjugal love that images God, or its perennial counterfeit—lust?

God is the one who united marital love and procreation. Therefore, since God cannot contradict himself, a "true contradiction cannot exist between the divine laws pertaining to the transmission of life and those pertaining to the fostering of authentic conjugal love" (GS, n. 51). It may well be difficult to follow the teaching of *Humanae Vitae*, but it could never be a contradiction of love.

Following this teaching is difficult because of the internal battle we all experience between love and lust. Lust impels us, and impels us very powerfully, towards sexual intercourse. But, as the future Pope observed in *Love & Responsibility*, if sexual intimacy results from nothing more than lust, it's not love. "On the contrary," he says, it "is a negation of ... love" (LR, 150-151). In reality, what we often call love, "if subjected to searching critical examination turns out to be, contrary to all appearances, only a form of 'utilization' of the person" (LR, p. 167).

What purpose does contraception really serve? This might sound odd at first, but let it sink in. Contraception was not invented to prevent pregnancy. We already had a 100% safe, 100% reliable way of doing that—*abstinence*. In the final analysis, contraception serves one purpose: to spare us the difficulty we experience when confronted with the choice of abstinence. When all the smoke is cleared, contraception was invented because of our lack of self-control; contraception was invented to serve the indulgence of lust.

Why do we spay or neuter our dogs and cats? Because they can't say no to their urge to merge; they're not free. If we spay and neuter ourselves with contraception, we're reducing the "great mystery" of the one flesh union to the level of Fido and Fidette in heat. What distinguished us from the animals in the first place (remember original solitude)? *Freedom!* God gave us freedom as the capacity to love. Contraception negates this freedom. It says, "I can't abstain." Hence, contracepted intercourse not only attacks the procreative meaning of sex, it "ceases also to be an act of love" (Aug. 22, 1984). If you can't say no to sex, what does your "yes" mean? Only the person who is *free* with the freedom for which Christ set us free (see Gal 5:1) is capable of authentic love.

Chastity and the Integration of Love

Chastity, so often considered "negative" or "repressive," is supremely positive and liberating. It's the virtue that frees sexual desire from "the utilitarian attitude," from the tendency to *use* others for our own gratification. Chastity requires "an *apprenticeship in self-mastery* which is training in human freedom. The alternative is clear: either man governs his passions and finds peace, or he lets himself be dominated by them and becomes unhappy" (CCC, n. 2339).

As we learned in chapter 3, self-mastery doesn't merely mean resisting unruly desires by force of will. That's only the "negative" side of the picture. As we develop self-mastery, we experience it as "the ability to direct [sexual] reactions, both as to their content and their character" (Oct. 31, 1984). The person who is truly chaste is able to direct erotic desire "towards the true, good, and beautiful—so that what is 'erotic' also becomes true, good, and beautiful" (Nov. 12, 1980). As spouses experience liberation from lust, they enter into the freedom of the gift which enables them to express "the 'language of the body' in a depth, simplicity, and beauty hitherto altogether unknown" (July 4, 1984).

It's certainly true that chastity requires "asceticism," understood as a ready and determined willingness to resist the impulses of lust. But, remember, authentic chastity doesn't repress. It enters into Christ's death and resurrection. As lust dies, authentic love is raised up. As the Pope expresses, "If conjugal chastity (and chastity in general) is manifested at first as the capacity to resist [lust], it later gradually reveals itself as a singular capacity to perceive, love, and practice those meanings of the 'language of the body' which remain altogether unknown to [lust] itself." Hence, the asceticism required by chastity doesn't impoverish or impede a couple's expressions of love and affection. Rather, it "makes them spiritually more intense and therefore enriches them" (Oct. 24, 1984).

Marital Spirituality

Such chastity, the Pope says, lies at "the center of the spirituality of marriage" (Nov. 14, 1984). What is "marital spirituality"? It's living according to God's in-spiration in married life. It involves spouses opening themselves to the indwelling power of the Holy Spirit and allowing him to guide them in all their choices and behaviors. The Pope says that sexual union itself—with all its emotional joys and physical pleasures—is meant to be an expression of "life according to the Holy Spirit" (see Dec. 1, 1982). When spouses are open to the gift, the Holy Spirit impregnates their sexual desires "with everything that is noble and beautiful," with "the supreme value, which is love" (Oct. 29, 1980). But when spouses, because of their "hardness of heart," close themselves off to the Holy Spirit, sexual union quickly degenerates into an act of lust, an act of mutual exploitation.

Apart from the Holy Spirit, human weakness makes the teaching of *Humanae Vitae* a burden no one can bear. But to whom is this teaching given? To men and women enslaved by their weaknesses? Or to men and women set free by the *power* of the Holy Spirit? This is what is at stake in the teaching of *Humanae Vitae*—the power of the Gospel! The Church holds out the teaching of *Humanae Vitae* with absolute confidence in the fact that "God's love has been poured into our hearts through the Holy Spirit who has been given to us" (Rom 5:5).

Married couples "must implore this essential 'power' by prayer; ... they must draw grace and love from the ever-living fountain of the Eucharist; ... they must overcome 'with humble perseverance' their deficiencies and sins in the sacrament of Penance." John Paul observes that these "are the means—*infallible and indispensable*—for forming the Christian spirituality of married life and family life" (Oct. 3, 1984). All of which, of course, presupposes faith, that openness of the human heart to the gift of the Holy Spirit.

If spouses are not living an authentic spirituality—in other words, if their hearts are closed to the transforming power of the Holy Spirit—they will inevitably view the Church's teaching against contraception as an oppressive rule to follow. On the other hand, for couples who engage in their sexual embrace as an expression of "life according to the Holy Spirit," rendering their union sterile becomes unthinkable. They understand that their union is meant to signify Christ's life-giving love for the Church. In other words, they understand the theology of their bodies. Filled "with veneration for the *essential values of the conjugal union*" (Nov. 14, 1984), they are ready and willing to make every sacrifice necessary so that lust does not trump love.

I'm far from being a perfect man and a perfect husband, but this vision of marital spirituality is *real* to me. As I already said, at one point I almost left the Church because of her teaching against contraception. I saw it as an oppressive, arbitrary ethic. But when I finally let go of my stubborn pride and prayed, "Okay, God, if this is true, you gotta change my heart," go figure, God started changing my heart. I gradually came to experience the "ethos of redemption." For those who live an authentic Christian ethos, the idea of engaging in contracepted intercourse becomes repulsive. Such people are free from the law! It doesn't feel imposed on them. It wells up from within as an expression of "life according to the Spirit." When such a change takes place in a person's heart, he begins to understand why the martyrs preferred to die rather than to break God's law. Again, I'm not perfect, but I can attest to this transformation. And if this change is possible in my life, it is possible in anyone's life.

The Antithesis of Marital Spirituality

The Pope observes that life in the Holy Spirit leads couples to a profound awe and respect for the mystery of God revealed in their bodies. It leads couples to understand, among all the possible manifestations of love and affection "the singular, or rather exceptional significance" of the sexual embrace (see Nov. 21, 1984).

Contraceptive practice—and the mentality behind it—demonstrates a total lack of understanding of the exceptional significance of the sexual embrace in God's plan. Such a lack, the Pope says, in a certain sense constitutes "the antithesis" of marital spirituality (see Nov. 21, 1984). If marital spirituality involves spouses opening their bodies—and the "one body" they become in the sexual act—to the Holy Spirit, contraception marks a specific "closing off" to the Holy Spirit. Who is the Holy Spirit? As we say in the Nicene Creed every Sunday, he's "the Lord, the Giver of Life." Contraception says, "Lord and Giver of Life, we don't want you here."

Isn't such a denial much like the original sin all over again? In the act of creation, God had "in-spired" the human body with his own life and love (see Gn 2: 7). When man and woman sinned, they "ex-spired"; they breathed God's Spirit *out* of their bodies. Or, you might say, they refused the Spirit's penetration because of their "hardness of heart." So, once again, I appeal to you: If today you hear his voice, harden not your hearts! (Heb 3:15).

Sexual union, right from the beginning, was meant to participate in God's eternal exchange of love. Do you know what couples actually say with their bodies when they close their union to the Lord and Giver of Life? In short, whether they realize this or not, contracepted intercourse says, "We prefer the momentary pleasure of a sterlized orgasm over the opportunity of participating in the inner-life of the Trinity." To which I respond, "*Bad choice!*" But do you think if couples really knew they were choosing this, that they would continue to do so? I can't help but think of Christ's words from the cross, "Father, forgive them; for they know not what they do" (Lk 23:34).

There is no tragedy in admitting we have sinned. There is no tragedy in admitting we have been duped by a counterfeit and sold a "pill" of goods. The only tragedy is the hardness of heart that refuses to admit its own sin. Be not afraid! As we've said so many times throughout this book, Christ came not to condemn, he came to save (see Jn 3:17). It doesn't matter how much lust has dominated your life. It doesn't matter how "dyslexic" or even "illiterate" you've been in reading the divine language of the body. As John Paul II boldly proclaims, through the gift of redemption "there always remains the possibility of passing from 'error' to the 'truth'...the possibility of ...conversion from sin to chastity as an expression of a life according to the Spirit" (Feb. 9, 1983).

Come, Holy Spirit, come! Convert our hearts from lust to love. Impregnate our sexual desires with divine passion so that, loving as God loves on earth, we might one day rejoice in the consummation of the "marriage of the Lamb" in heaven. Amen.

Chapter 8

SHARING THE THEOLOGY OF THE BODY IN A "NEW EVANGELIZATION"

At "the core of [the] Gospel ... is the affirmation of the inseparable connection between the person, his life and his bodiliness."
—John Paul II (EV, n. 81)

If the future of humanity passes by way of marriage and the family (see FC, n. 11), we could say that the future of marriage and the family passes by way of John Paul II's theology of the body. Put simply, there will be no renewal of the Church and of the world without a renewal of marriage and the family. And there will be no renewal of marriage and the family without a return to the full truth of God's plan for the body and sexuality. Yet this won't happen without a fresh theological proposal that compellingly demonstrates how the Christian sexual ethic—far from the cramped, prudish list of prohibitions it's assumed to be—is a liberating message of salvation that corresponds perfectly with the yearnings of the human heart.

This is precisely what John Paul II's theology of the body offers us. As such it provides the antidote to the culture of death and a theological foundation for the "new evangelization."

What is the New Evangelization?

John Paul first used the expression "the new evangelization" in a trip to Latin America in 1983. Ever since he has "unstintingly recalled the pressing need for a *new evangelization*" (FR, n. 103). This urgency stems not only from the fact that entire nations still haven't received the Gospel, but also because "entire groups of the baptized have lost a living sense of the faith, or even no longer consider themselves members of the Church, and live a life far removed from Christ and his Gospel" (RM, n. 86).

Therefore, one thing "new" about this evangelization is that it's directed in large part towards "baptized non-believers." Men and women in large numbers are "culturally Christian," but haven't experienced a conversion of heart to Christ and his teachings. The call to interior conversion, in fact, was one of the main themes of Vatican II. As the Council understood well, this can only happen through an authentic, compelling, evangelical witness to salvation through Jesus Christ.

As John Paul clarified in his Apostolic Letter *At the Beginning of the New Millennium*, the new evangelization isn't "a matter of inventing a 'new program.' The program already exists: it is the plan found in the Gospel and in the living Tradition, it is the same as ever" (n. 29). What's essential in order to bring the Gospel to the modern world is a proclamation that's "new in ardor, methods, and expression" (March 9, 1983).

Speaking to the American Bishops in 1998, the Pope observed that "*the new evangelization* [involves] a vital effort to come to a deeper understanding of the mysteries of faith and to find meaningful language with which to convince our contemporaries that they are called to newness of life through God's love." It's the task of sharing with modern men and women "the 'unsearchable riches of Christ' and of making known 'the plan of the mystery hidden for ages in God who created all things' (Eph 3:8-9)" (SE, 53, 55).

"How am I supposed to do that?" you ask. Here's a suggestion: talk about sex. What a great starting point for evangelization—everybody's interested! I say this with a bit of humor, but I'm also entirely serious. If we're to make known to others "the plan of the mystery hidden for ages in God," as we have learned throughout this book, there's an image of this mystery stamped right in our sexuality. The theology of the body provides just the "meaningful language" we need "to convince our contemporaries that they are called to newness of life through God's love."

Bringing Heavenly Mysteries Down to Earth

Wouldn't you agree that the Pope's theology of the body—once it's presented in a way that people can understand—has a remarkable ability to bring the heavenly mysteries down to earth? The Pope's insights "ring true" because his teaching is the fruit of a constant confrontation of doctrine with experience.

As the Holy Father observes, "God comes to us in the things we know best and can verify most easily, the things of our everyday life, apart from which we cannot understand ourselves" (FR, n. 12). What do we know better, what can we verify more easily, what's more "every day" than the experience of embodiment? This is where God meets us—*in the flesh*. And this is where we must meet the world in the new evangelization.

The *Catechism* teaches that the Church "in her whole being and in all her members ...is sent to announce, bear witness, make present, and spread the mystery of the communion of the Holy Trinity" (n. 738). This sums up well the essential goal of evangelization. And this eternal mystery of *communion* becomes close to us, we realize that it's part of us through the lens of the theology of the body. The mystery of love and communion isn't something "out there" somewhere. It's "right here"—stamped in our whole personal experience of "being a body," of being male or female.

Our creation as male and female and our longing for communion is "the fundamental fact" of human existence (see Feb. 13, 1980). Again, the Gospel meets us right here. As John Paul says, the Christian mystery cannot be understood "unless we keep in mind the 'great mystery' involved in the creation of man as male and female and the vocation of both to conjugal love" (LF, n. 19).

Incarnating the Gospel

In that same address to the American Bishops quoted above, John Paul defined the basic task of evangelization as "the Church's effort to proclaim to [all men and women] that God loves them, that he has given himself for them in Christ Jesus, and that he invites them to an unending life of happiness" (SE, 55). This basic message is in itself "good news." But it needs to be *incarnated* if men and women are to find their link with it.

Of course, this message was and *is* incarnated in Jesus Christ. But can't you just hear one of your friends or neighbors saying, "What does some man who lived two thousand years ago have to do with me?" As a professor of mine used to say, we can proclaim that "Jesus is the *answer*" til we're blue in the face. But unless people are first in touch with the *question*, we remain on the level of abstraction.

Herein lies the gift of grounding the Gospel in the body. It's the antidote to abstraction. It roots us in what's truly human—in the "every day"—and by so doing prepares us to receive what's truly divine. In other words, it puts us squarely in touch with the human question, thus opening our hearts to the divine answer.

In some sense, embodiment *is* the human question. What does it mean to be a man? What does it mean to be a woman? There are no more important questions for men and women to ask. And notice that these are inherently sexual questions, questions about "being a body."

Human Longing Leads to Christ

Of course, the very ability to question and to wonder flows from our deeper, spiritual dimension. But as we've learned throughout this book, the human anomaly is that our *spiritual* dimension is manifested in our *physical* dimension.

It was *in his body* that Adam realized he was "alone" in the world and that it was not good to be so. We're meant for love, for communion with an "other." This is what the body teaches us: we're destined for love. As John Paul II states so eloquently: "Man cannot live without love. He remains a being that is incomprehensible for himself, his life is senseless, if love is not revealed to him, if he does not encounter love, if he does experience it and make it his own, if he does not participate intimately in it. This ... is why Christ the Redeemer 'fully reveals man to himself'" (RH, n. 10)—because his body "given up for us" reveals the truth about incarnate love.

The call to "incarnate love" isn't abstract. Even if sin has distanced us from the beauty and purity of God's original plan, everyone knows the "ache" of solitude and the longing for communion. Everyone knows the "magnetic pull" of erotic desire. This basic human longing for union, in fact, is the most concrete link in every human heart with "that man who lived two thousand years ago." For all human longing, when purified, leads us to Christ, and none more so than the longing to unite with an "other" in the sexual embrace. "For this reason ...the two become one flesh." For what reason? To reveal, proclaim, and anticipate the union of Christ and the Church (see Eph 5:31-32).

The eternal, ecstatic, "nuptial" Communion with Christ and the entire communion of saints—so far superior to anything proper to earthly life that we can't begin to fathom it—this alone can satisfy the human "ache" of solitude. This is the North Pole to which that magnetic pull of erotic desire is oriented. Borrowing an idea from St. Augustine, we're made for communion with Christ, and our hearts are restless until we rest in this eternal embrace.

The Task of the New Evangelization

Sin's tactic is simply to "twist" and "disorient" our desire for heaven, our desire for Christ's eternal union with the Church. Recall our earlier observation that the sexual confusion so prevalent in our world and in our own hearts is nothing but the human desire for heaven gone berserk. The task of the new evangelization, then, isn't to condemn the world for its excesses and distortions, but to help the world "untwist" them.

As the early Christian writer Tertullian said, the devil seeks to counter God's plan by plagiarizing the sacraments. That's all he can do—take what God created for our joy and happiness (the sacraments) and put his own branding on it. For example, the typical American college student quickly learns that the meaning of life is to get drunk and have rampant sex. "Untwist" these counterfeits and you discover two sacraments: the Eucharist and marriage.

We're meant to be "inebriated" on the new wine that Christ gives us. And where did Christ first reveal the gift of this new wine? At a wedding feast (see John 2). The union of the sexes can only bring us the joy we seek if it images Christ's love poured out in the Eucharist. This is what we really long for. In the new evangelization, we need to be able to walk into fraternity parties where people are getting drunk and seeking illicit sex and say, "Do you know what you really want here? You want the Eucharist and marriage, and the Catholic Church has them in their fullness."

Once again I'm inserting a bit of humor. But again, I'm also serious. Behind every sin, behind every disordered "acting out," there's a genuine human desire that's meant to be fulfilled through Christ and his Church. As our desires become "untwisted," we begin to realize that we really desire eternal love and joy. This is what we're created for. And the good news of the Gospel is that just such a love has been revealed. It's already been freely given. How? Where? In *the body* of Christ. *This* is why "Jesus is the answer."

If the spirit of the Gospel isn't *incarnated* in this way with men and women's real desires, it will forever remain detached from what we experience as "essentially human." Yet, Christ took on flesh to wed himself to what's essentially human. Hence, if the Gospel isn't incarnated with what's essentially human, it's essentially not the Gospel of Jesus Christ.

The Gospel of the Body

The "core of the Gospel," according to John Paul, "is the proclamation of a living God who is close to us, who calls us to profound communion with himself .... It is the affirmation of the inseparable connection between the person, his life and his bodiliness. It is the presentation of human life as a life of relationship." As a consequence, the Pope says that "the meaning of life is found in giving and receiving love, and in this light human sexuality and procreation reach their true and full significance" (EV, n. 81).

We might call this profoundly incarnate vision the "gospel of the body." In a word, the Gospel is a call to communion. This is what we long for and this is what our bodies shout: *communion!* As John Paul asserts in his letter on the new millennium, "To make the Church *the home and school of communion*: that is the great challenge facing us in the millennium which is now beginning, if we wish to be faithful to God's plan and respond to the world's deepest yearnings" (NMI, n. 43).

But we can only pass on this good news of love and communion—this "gospel of the body"—if we're first infused with it and vivified by it ourselves. As Pope Paul VI said in his great letter *On Evangelization in the Modern World*, "The Church is an evangelizer, but she begins by being evangelized herself" (n. 15). There's no doubt that, in delivering his theology of the body, John Paul II's intended audience was, first and foremost, the Church herself.

Very few Christians seem to understand that an image of the Gospel is stamped in their own bodies and in their yearning for union. Large numbers of Catholics have been caught up in the counterfeits of the day and are hostile towards the Church's teaching. Hence, unless the tide is turned within the Church—unless the Church is first evangelized—she cannot evangelize others.

The Spousal Analogy & the "Analogy of Faith"

John Paul II's theology of the body provides great hope for this urgently needed renewal within the Church. When we view the Gospel message through the interpretive key of man and woman's call to communion, not only does the Gospel message take on flesh, but even the most controversial teachings of the Church—contraception, divorce and remarriage, homosexuality, an all-male priesthood, etc.—begin to make beautiful sense.

Spousal theology demonstrates how all of the various puzzle pieces of the Christian mystery fit perfectly together. The truth of Catholicism "clicks" when viewed through the theology of the body. In other words, through the spousal analogy we become attentive to the "analogy of faith"—that is, to the coherence of the truths of faith among themselves and within the whole plan of Revelation centered on Christ (see CCC, nn. 90, 114, 158).

This is why the theology of the body will lead to a dramatic development of thinking about the tenets of our Creed. This is why the *Catechism* speaks of the important connection between sexual rectitude, believing in the articles of the Creed, and *understanding* the mysteries we profess in the Creed. In other words, the *Catechism* points to the intimate connection between purity of heart, love of the truth, and orthodoxy of faith (see n. 2518).

Conversely, as the last few decades of dissent demonstrate, Christianity unravels at the seams—its inner logic collapses and so many of its core beliefs become contested—as soon as we divorce ourselves from the "great mystery" of nuptial communion revealed through the body.

In Conclusion

Returning to an image we used previously, comparing John Paul II's grand vision of human sexuality to the impoverished vision we find in today's media is like comparing the luscious food at an elaborate banquet to the maggot-ridden scraps found at the bottom of a dumpster. And, yet, for lack of knowledge that such a banquet even exists—and that all without exception are invited to partake—our world continues to feed its hunger for love with such scraps. *Woe to us if we do not proclaim the Gospel of the body from the rooftops! Woe to us if we do not invite everyone to the banquet!*

Only a microscopic percentage of people on this planet have been exposed to the good news of the theology of the body. You are now one of them. What will you do with the scattered seeds that have fallen to you? I appeal to you, do not let the birds of the air eat them. Do not let the seeds die for lack of moisture. Do not let the cares of this world choke them off (see Lk 8: 4-15). Tend to the soil and water the seeds by taking up a further, more in-depth study of the Pope's theology of the body (see the resource section). Make it your mission in life to understand it, live it, and share it with everyone you know.

Understanding, living, and sharing the truth of your masculinity or femininity is not "yet another task" to add to your Christian life. Living according to the truth of our embodiment as male and female takes us to the heart of the Christian life. Remember that the theology of the body "concerns the entire Bible" (Jan 13, 1982) and plunges us into "the perspective of the whole Gospel, of the whole teaching, in fact, of the whole mission of Christ" (Dec 3, 1980).

If the theology of the body provides the answer to the crisis of our times, it does so only because it reconnects the modern world with the "great mystery" of Christ and his Church. As John Paul II writes, "We are certainly not seduced by the naive expectation that, faced with the great challenges of our time, we shall find some magic formula. No, we shall not be saved by a formula, but by a Person, and the assurance which he gives us: *I am with you!*" (NMI, n. 29). Christ the Bridegroom is with us! (see LF, part II)

This is our living hope. This is the hope that John Paul II offers us in his theology of the body. If we share this hope with the world, together, we shall not fall short of renewing the face of the earth.

Let it be, Lord, according to your will. Mary, woman of glory and star of the new evangelization, pray for us. Amen.

GLOSSARY

This glossary provides partial definitions of key terms and phrases for quick reference. Terms and phrases are listed in the order in which they appear in this book. In this way the glossary also serves as a summary of the book.

Chapter 1 – What is the Theology of the Body?

1. *Theology of the body*: The study of how God reveals his mystery through the human body. This is also the title of John Paul II's 129 short talks on the subject.

2. *Incarnation*: The doctrine that refers to the Eternal Word, the second Person of the Holy Trinity, taking on human flesh and being born of a woman.

3. *Manichaeism*: An ancient dualistic heresy credited to Mani (or Manichaeus) that posits the source of evil in matter and therefore condemns the body and sex.

4. *Sacrament*: In its more ancient meaning, this refers to a physical sign that makes visible what is invisible. In its more strict meaning, sacrament refers to the seven signs of the new covenant (baptism, confirmation, Eucharist, penance, anointing of the sick, holy orders, marriage) instituted by Christ to confer the grace of redemption.

5. *Spiritualized body*: Refers to the fact that the human body is "in breathed" not only with a spiritual soul but also, through the grace of redemption, with God's Holy Spirit.

6. *Divine mystery*: Refers to the two-fold "inner secret" of God: first, that God exists as a Trinity of persons in an eternal "exchange of love" and, second, that God has destined man (male and female) to participate in this exchange of love.

7. *Communion of persons*: Refers to the unity or "common union" established when persons mutually give and receive "the sincere gift of self." The male-female communion of persons in marriage is a created image of *the* Communion of Persons found in the Trinity.

8. *Sincere self-giving*: Christ demonstrates that love is realized in and through self-donation. To say that man can only find himself through the "sincere gift of self" is to say that man can only realize who he is by loving as Christ loves.

9. *Spousal analogy*: Refers to the scriptural use of marital love as an earthly image of God's love for Israel and, in the New Testament, Christ's love for the Church. Like all analogies, the spousal analogy is inadequate in communicating God's infinitely transcendent mystery. Yet, according to John Paul II, it is the most fitting human image of the divine mystery.

10. *Spiritual battle*: Refers to the conflict between good and evil that rages in us and all around us. The union of the sexes finds itself at the center of this great contest.

11. *Culture of death*: Refers to the utilitarian cultural milieu in which persons not only are treated as a means to an end, but—if they don't serve a given end—they are disregarded, mistreated, or even eliminated.

12. *Culture of life*: Refers to the cultural milieu in which human life is respected as the greatest of all gifts and every sacrifice is made to uphold each person's inestimable worth and value.

Chapter 2 – Before the Fig Leaves: God's Original Plan for the Body & Sex

13. *Original solitude*: Refers not only to Adam's experience of being "alone" without a helper, but also to the human experience of being "alone" in the visible world as a person made in God's image and likeness. Adam discovered his solitude by naming the animals and realizing he was fundamentally different from them.

14. *Freedom*: The capacity to *choose* and *determine* one's own actions. This is the main distinction between the human person and the animals.

15. *Person / subject*: These terms designate man's "greatness," the fact that he has an "inner life," an "inner self." Man is not merely some*thing* but some*one*.

16. *Knowledge of good and evil*: Man has the capacity to distinguish between good and evil, but he is not free to determine what is good and what is evil.

17. *Original unity*: Refers to man and woman's experience of self-donating love and communion prior to sin. This unity resolved solitude in the sense of being without a "helper," but affirmed human solitude in the sense of being different from the animals. The original unity of man and woman in "one flesh" is worlds apart from the copulation of animals.

18. *Sacramentality of the body*: Refers to the body's capacity of making visible what is invisible. The body proclaims a "great mystery"—the spiritual mystery of God's Trinitarian love and our call to share in that love through Christ.

19. *Communion of persons* (see # 7 above)

20. *Primordial sacrament*: Refers to marriage as the original and fundamental revelation of God's mystery in the created world.

21. *Original nakedness*: Refers to the original experience of nakedness without shame. Adam and Eve were untainted by shame because they had no experience whatsoever of lust. Before sin, man and woman experienced sexual desire as the desire to love in God's image.

22. *Shame*: In its negative sense, shame indicates that we have lost sight of the dignity and goodness of the body as a "theology"—a revelation of God's mystery. In its positive sense, shame indicates a desire to protect the goodness of the body from the degradation of lust.

23. *Lust*: Refers to sexual desire void of God's love. Lust leads a person toward *self-gratification* at the expense of the other, while love leads a person toward *self-donation* for the good of the other. Lust, therefore, is a *reduction* of the original fullness God intended for the sexual relationship.

24. *Interior gaze*: Refers to the "pure look" that Adam and Eve freely exchanged with one another in the state of innocence. It indicates not only a seeing of the body with

the eyes, but through that physical vision they were able to gaze upon the interior truth of the person.

25. *Freedom of the gift*: This indicates that, prior to sin, man and woman did not experience sexual desire as a compulsion or uncontrollable urge. They were totally free and in this freedom they desired only to be a gift to each other. We are called in Christ to reclaim this freedom. It is for freedom that Christ has set us free (see Gal 5:1).

26. *The original good of God's vision*: Taken from Genesis 1: 31 ("God saw everything that he had made, and behold, it was very good."), this refers to the fact that everything God created is fundamentally good. Consequently, evil is not a reality in its own right, but is only and always a deprivation or reduction of the good that God created.

27. *Holiness*: Refers to the state of the person who loves rightly. God's holiness is manifested in his eternal exchange of self-giving love. Human holiness is what enables us to image God through the sincere gift of self. For the human person, as for the Incarnate Christ, holiness is manifested in and through the human body.

28. *Nuptial love*: Refers to the love of "total self-donation." Marriage provides a model of such love, but it is not the only way of expressing the total gift of self.

29. *The nuptial meaning of the body*: Refers to the call to love as God loves inscribed in the human body as male and female. If we live according to the nuptial meaning of our bodies, we fulfill the very meaning of our being and existence (see #28 above).

30. *Universal call to holiness*: Refers to the fact that God calls everyone, without exception, to "love as he loves" through the sincere gift of self.

Chapter 3 – The Entrance of the Fig Leaves: The Effects of Sin and the Redemption of Sexuality

31. *Adultery committed in the heart*: This is committed when a person decides inwardly to treat another human being as an object to gratify lust rather than as a person to love in the image of God.

32. *The heritage of our hearts*: Refers to those deeper dispositions of our hearts that we have "inherited" not only through sin, but, more deeply, from the original experiences of man and woman. The heritage of our hearts goes deeper than lust and we still desire what is deeper; we still desire authentic love. Christ empowers us to live from that deeper heritage of our hearts.

33. *Questioning the gift*: Refers to the doubt that entered the human heart regarding God's disposition towards us. God's true disposition is one of self-donation ("gift"). With the dawn of sin we came to conceive of God, rather, as a tyrant who was withholding that which we desired.

34. *The second discovery of sex*: Refers to the experience after original sin in which the sexual relationship degenerated from one of love and communion to one of lust and domination.

35. *Lust* (see # 23 above)

36. *Shame* (see # 22 above)

37. *A living morality*: Refers to the "life" Christ offers us that enables and empowers us to desire and freely choose that which is true, good, and beautiful. It is to be distinguished from a sterile or "lifeless" approach to morality that, because of the allurement of evil, views God's law as a burden and an impediment.

38. *Ethic and ethos*: An ethic is an objective moral law or command. *Ethos*, on the other hand, refers to the abiding inner desires of the heart—what attracts and repulses a person. In the Sermon on the Mount, Christ demonstrates that the ethic is not enough ("You have heard the command...but I tell you..."). Christ came to transform our *ethos*, to change our hearts.

39. *The ethos of redemption* (also, *Christian ethos*, or *new ethos*): This is characterized by a transformation of the human heart such as to desire and to realize God's original plan for human life and the union of the sexes.

40. *Freedom from the law*: This is realized when, through the ethos of redemption, the heart is transformed to the point that it no longer needs "the law" (the ethic) because it does not desire to break it.

41. *Grace*: God's love poured into the human heart through the Holy Spirit. Grace enables men and women to "become who they are," to live and love as God intends. Grace penetrates the whole human person, body and soul, and enables us to "give up our bodies" through the sincere gift of self.

42. *Faith*: In its deepest essence, faith is the openness of the human heart to God's grace, to the divine gift, to the love poured into the human heart through the Holy Spirit.

43. *The grace of creation*: Refers to the gift of God's love poured out in the creation of the world and, in particular, the creation of man and woman. This grace enabled the first human couple to love one another in the divine image before the fall.

44. *The grace of redemption*: Refers to the gift of God's love poured out in the redemption of the world and, in particular, the redemption of man and woman. This grace enables men and women—to the degree that they take up their crosses and follow Christ—gradually to reclaim God's original plan and live it. The grace of redemption will come to total fulfillment in the resurrection of the body.

45. *Life according to the Spirit*: Refers to a life infused with the grace of redemption, that is, the life of the Holy Spirit. To the degree that we live "according to the Spirit" we are free from the law because our hearts conform to the law. Living according to the Spirit does *not* mean we reject our bodies; it means we open our bodies to the Holy Spirit's inspiration.

46. *Life according to the flesh*: Refers to a life cut off from divine inspiration. Such a person is bound by lust and the other vices and so experiences God's law as a burden and imposition. This does not mean our flesh is "bad," but that our flesh needs to be inspired, that is, filled with God's Spirit.

47. *The redemption of the body*: To the degree that we experience "life according to the Spirit" we also experience the redemption of our bodies. This refers to the restoration of the human person in his or her integrity as a unity of body and soul. It affords the

recovery of God's original plan in the human heart. This redemption is not only something we hope for in the resurrection from the dead. It is already at work in us within history.

48. *Purity of heart*: To the degree that we are pure of heart we understand, see, and experience the body as God created it to be, as a revelation of his own divine mystery. "Blessed are the pure in heart, for they shall see God" (Mt 5:8).

49. *The interpretation of suspicion*: Those who live by this interpretation remain so locked in their own lusts that they project the same bondage onto everyone else. They cannot imagine any way to think about the human body and the sexual relationship other than through the prism of lust. This view is the antithesis of the meaning of life.

Chapter 4 – Beyond the Fig Leaves: The Resurrection of the Body

50. *The resurrection of the body*: The doctrine that the human body is also destined for everlasting life in union with the human soul. Eternal life is not only a "spiritual" reality. Man (male and female) is destined to share in the life of the Trinity as a body-person.

51. *The spiritualization of the body*: In the resurrection the body will be completely "spiritualized," which means not only the perfect integrity of body and soul, but also the perfect "indwelling" of the human body-person by the Holy Spirit (see also # 5 above).

52. *The divinization of the body*: Since it is the divine Person of the Holy Spirit that will permeate the human

body in the resurrection, the body will be in some way "divinized" or made divine. What God is by nature, we will participate in by grace. We will not lose our human nature, but through God's utterly gratuitous gift, men and women will participate—body and soul—in the divine nature (see 2 Pt 1:4).

53. *The Marriage of the Lamb*: The image used by the book of Revelation to describe the eternal union of Christ and the Church. Christ, the unblemished "Lamb of God," will forever make a gift of himself to his Bride, the Church, and the Church will return the gift of herself to Christ. Through this mutual exchange of love, God and man will live in eternal communion.

54. *The beatific vision*: The eternal vision of God granted to those who respond to the wedding invitation of the Lamb. The unsurpassed beauty and splendor of this eternal vision of God will fill all who behold with never-ending bliss.

55. *Fulfillment of the nuptial meaning of the body*: In the resurrection, the nuptial meaning of the body will be definitively revealed and fulfilled in receiving God's self-gift and returning the gift of self to God.

56. *Communion of saints*: Not only will the saints in heaven live in eternal communion with God, they will also live in eternal communion with each other. There already exists a communion between those in heaven and those still journeying toward heaven on earth. In the resurrection, this communion of saints will fulfill definitively the unity of the human race which God willed from the beginning.

Chapter 5 – Christian Celibacy: A Marriage Made in Heaven

57. *Eunuch*: Someone physically incapable of sexual intercourse.

58. *Eunuch for the kingdom of heaven*: Someone who chooses freely to forgo sexual intercourse in order to devote himself or herself totally to the "marriage of the Lamb."

59. *The "superiority" of celibacy*: This vocation is "better" not because of celibacy itself, but because the heavenly marriage (to which celibates devote themselves more directly) is objectively superior to the earthly marriage. Subjectively speaking, the "better" vocation is the one to which a given person is called.

60. *Manichaeism* (see # 3 above)

61. *Complementarity of vocations*: Refers to the fact that Christian celibacy and Christian marriage do not conflict or compete with each other; rather, they enrich and complement each other. Marriage reveals the "nuptial" character of celibacy just as celibacy reveals the sacramental orientation of marriage.

62. *Celibacy expresses the nuptial meaning of the body*: Christian celibacy involves no rejection of the body and sexuality, but expresses the ultimate purpose and meaning of the body and sexuality by pointing so profoundly to the marriage of the Lamb. The celibate man or woman expresses the nuptial meaning of the body by becoming a sincere gift to others. This leads, in turn, to a spiritual fruitfulness.

Chapter 6 – Christian Marriage: Imaging Christ's Union with the Church

63. *Mutual submission*: The Apostle Paul makes use of the language of "submission" common in his day, but he exhorts spouses to a revolutionary understanding of it. Submission in Christian marriage is *mutual* and modeled not according to lust and domination, but according to the image of Christ and his Church.

64. *Reverence for Christ*: Spouses must submit to one another "out of reverence for Christ." This is nothing other than a spiritually mature form of the mutual attraction of the sexes. To the degree that we experience the redemption of sexual desire, the beauty of the opposite sex elicits not lust, but a deep awe and respect.

65. *Headship*: According to the "head and body" analogy employed by St. Paul, the husband is the head and the wife the body. The husband's headship calls him not to domination and authoritarian control, but to be the first to serve, to lay down his life for his bride (and children) in imitation of Christ.

66. *Sacramentality of the body* (see # 18 above)

67. *Sacrament of creation*: Refers to the fact that God's "mystery of love" became most visible in creation through the "sign" of the union between man and woman.

68. *Sacrament of redemption*: Refers to the fact that God's "mystery of love" is definitively revealed in redemption through the "sign" of Christ's union with the Church, which St. Paul compares to the nuptial union of spouses.

69. *The language of the body*: Refers to the body's capacity to "speak" or "proclaim" God's love. It does so—or is meant to do so—most profoundly in the "one flesh" union of spouses. Here spouses are meant to renew their marriage vows with their bodies.

70. *Agape*: The Greek word for divine love. Christ's love is *free, total, faithful,* and *fruitful.* In Christian marriage, eros and agape are called to meet and bear fruit. If spouses are to be faithful to the "language of their bodies," sexual intercourse must express *agape.*

71. *The prophetism of the body*: The body is "prophetic" because it is meant to proclaim God's love. However, we must be careful to distinguish between true and false prophets. If we can speak the truth with the body, we can also speak lies.

Chapter 7 – Theology in the Bedroom: A Liberating Sexual Morality

72. *Humanae Vitae*: Translated as *Of Human Life,* this is the title of Pope Paul VI's 1968 encyclical letter reaffirming the constant teaching of the Church on the immorality of contraception.

73. *A total vision of man*: Pope Paul VI stated in *Humanae Vitae* that in order to understand the Church's teaching on sexual morality, we need to view it in light of a total vision of man and of his vocation. Who is man? Why does he exist and what is he destined for? It is this "total vision of man" that John Paul II sketches in his theology of the body.

74. *"My sister, my bride"*: This expression from the Song of Songs demonstrates that the lover recognizes that his

beloved shares the same humanity he does. Calling her "sister" *before* calling her "bride" indicates that his motive is not one of lust, but of sincere self-giving.

75. *"A garden enclosed"*: This expression from the Song of Songs indicates that the lover recognizes his beloved as "master of her own mystery." In other words, he sees and respects her dignity as an inviolable, self-determining person. The only way he can enter this "garden" is with her freely given "yes." If he were to manipulate her or barge through the door, he would violate her personhood.

76. *Test of life and death*: The marriage of Tobiah and Sarah indicates that joining in "one flesh" takes spouses to the center of the great contest between good and evil, between life and death. But love is confident in the victory and is ready to do everything so that life conquers death.

77. *Ethics of the sign*: The norm for sexual morality is whether or not a given behavior truly images or signifies the *free, total, faithful, fruitful* love of Christ. If it does not, it is a counterfeit for the love we truly desire.

78. *Responsible parenthood*: In the language of the Church, responsible parenthood is practiced by those who prudently and generously decide to have a large family or by those who—for a serious reason and with respect for the language of the body—seek to space and/or limit children.

79. *Natural family planning*: Refers to those methods of family planning that are in keeping with God's plan for fertility and marital love. Modern methods of natural family planning are to be distinguished from the older

and much less reliable "rhythm method." Modern methods of NFP are 98-99% effective at avoiding pregnancy when used properly and can be used by any woman, regardless of the regularity or irregularity of her cycles.

80. *Chastity*: The virtue that orients sexual desire toward the supreme value of the person and the truth of self-giving love.

81. *Marital spirituality*: "Life according to the Spirit" (see # 45 above) as applied to married life. It involves the openness of the spouses' bodies, and the "one body" they become, to the presence and indwelling of the Holy Spirit, the Lord and Giver of Life. Since contraception marks a "closing off" to the Lord and Giver of life, contraceptive practice and mentality are in some sense the "antithesis" of an authentic marital spirituality.

Chapter 8 – Sharing the Theology of the Body in a "New Evangelization"

82. *New evangelization*: Refers to the urgent need to proclaim the "great mystery" of Christ's love to the whole world. What's "new" about this evangelization is not the message. Rather, it is the fact that this evangelistic effort is directed largely towards "baptized non-believers." If the Church is to reach modern men and women with the Gospel, her proclamation must be "new in ardor, methods, and expression."

83. *Incarnating the Gospel*: This means demonstrating that God's plan of love for humanity is not "out there" somewhere. It's "right here" in our everyday experience of being male and female and in our longing for

communion. If the Gospel isn't *incarnated* in this way, it will forever remain detached from what is "essentially human." And if the Gospel isn't incarnated with what's essentially human, it's essentially not the Gospel of Jesus Christ.

84. *Incarnate love:* Love is supremely spiritual. The human paradox, however, is that the spiritual is manifested in the body. It is in *our bodies* that we experience the divine call to love and self-donation. This is why Christ "fully reveals man to himself"—because he reveals the truth about incarnate love by "giving up his body" for us.

85. *Gospel of the body:* If the Gospel is the "good news" of our salvation in Christ, the expression "Gospel of the body" indicates that the human body is a sign and instrument of the same message of our salvation in Christ. In a word, the Gospel is a call to communion. This is what our bodies shout as male and female: *communion!*—"and I mean in reference to Christ and the church" (Eph 5:32).

86. *Analogy of faith:* Refers to the coherence of the truths of faith among themselves and within the whole plan of God's Revelation. There is an inter-connectedness of the truths of faith, each one being integrally related to the others. The theology of the body helps demonstrate how the various puzzle pieces of the Christian mystery fit beautifully together.

RESOURCE SECTION

The following is a partial list of resources and organizations that can assist you in your further study of John Paul II's theology of the body.

Other Resources by Christopher West

Books
- *Good News About Sex & Marriage: Answers to Your Honest Questions about Catholic Teaching* (Servant, 2000)
- *Crash Course in the Theology of the Body: A Study Guide* (GIFT Foundation/Luminous Media, 2002)
- *Theology of the Body Explained: A Commentary on John Paul II's "Gospel of the Body"* (Pauline, 2003)

Audio & Video Presentations

- Christopher West has an extensive collection of audio and video presentations available for personal or group study. Visit christopherwest.com or luminousmedia.org for more information or call 800-376-0520.

Official Web Site

- Visit christopherwest.com or theologyofthebody.com for information on Christopher's speaking schedule, downloadable articles and sound files, or to purchase any of his books and other resources.

Books, Tapes, and Other Resources

The GIFT Foundation
- · This not-for-profit lay apostolate offers a variety of audio and video resources on the theology of the body, natural family planning, and related topics.
- · Visit giftfoundation.org or call 847-844-1167

Luminous Media
- · Luminous Media is Christopher West's official media company. They also carry audio and video products of other well-known Catholic speakers.
- · Visit luminousmedia.org or catholictalks.com. Or call 800-376-0520.

Our Father's Will Communications
- · Offers audio and video products by speakers like Katrina Zeno, David Sloan, Christopher West, and many more.
- · Visit theologyofthebody.net or call 866-333-OFWC.

Pauline Books and Media
- · Publishers of John Paul II's *Theology of the Body: Human Love in the Divine Plan* and Christopher West's *Theology of the Body Explained: A Commentary on John Paul II's "Gospel of the Body."*
- · Visit pauline.org or call 800-876-4463.

Real Love Productions
- · Books, videos and other resources by Mary Beth Bonacci. In her dynamic presentations, Mary Beth draws from the theology of the body to support teens, young adults, and parents in their

quest for a true understanding of what it means to love and be loved.

· Visit reallove.net or call 888-667-4992.

Organizations

Domestic-church.com

Family Honor
· Family Honor provides resources and programs based on the theology of the body to help parents and children grow together in their understanding of God's plan for life and human sexuality.
· Visit familyhonor.org or call 877-208-1353

Theology of the Body Foundation
· The Theology of the Body Foundation's mission is to promote and foster an understanding of the Theology of the Body throughout the world. It educates through books, pamphlets, audio and video recordings, seminars, a continuing education Institute, and media such as newspapers and magazines, television, radio and the Internet.
· Visit theologyofthebody.org

Theology of the Body Evangelization Team (TOBET)
· Engages in activities of evangelization, apologetics, education, charity and mission through the use of various media with a focus on Pope John Paul II's theology of the body.
· Visit tobet.org

Theology of the Body International Alliance (TOBIA)
· This is a support network providing resources for those striving to evangelize the world by means of Pope John Paul II's understanding of the human

person, explained in his works *Love and Responsibility* and *Theology of the Body.* Great resource for help in starting a study group.
- Visit theologyofthebody.net and click on "TOBIA"

Love and Responsibility Foundation
- This organization is dedicated to promoting the teachings of Pope John Paul II on marriage and the family.
- Visit catholicculture.com

Women Affirming Life
- Offers "A New Language" study series on the theology of the body by Professor Mary Shivanandan of the John Paul II Institute. This is a four-season group study series, each consisting of six weekly sessions.
- Visit affirmlife.com or call 617-254-2277.

Women of the Third Millennium (WTTM)
- This is a lay organization co-founded by Katrina Zeno and Zoe Romanowsky in response to John Paul II's call for women to develop a "new feminism." WTTM offers a variety of retreats for women and men.
- Visit wttm.org or call 740-282-9062.

Further Education/Training

Heart Mind and Strength University for Living (HMSU)
- HMSU offers online courses that are "part retreat, part seminar, part small faith group." Class size is strictly limited to ensure personal attention from your Instructor/Mentor as well as to afford plenty of opportunity to interact with

other learners. Courses in the theology of the body and related subjects are available.

· Visit HMSU.com.

John Paul II Institute for Studies on Marriage & Family

· This Pontifical Institute is a graduate school of theology founded by Pope John Paul II to help the Church understand more fully the human person, marriage and family in light of divine revelation. Campuses of the Institute exist in many countries throughout the world.

· Visit johnpaulii.edu for the American campus and jp2institute.org for the Australian campus.

Theology of the Body Summer Institute

· Beginning in the summer of 2004, this new initiative will offer credit and non-credit courses in the theology of the body and related subjects with the goal of equipping lay men and women, priests, seminarians, and religious to play a more active role in teaching and spreading John Paul II's theology of the body.

· Visit theologyofthebody.com and click on "Summer Institute" or call 610-696-7795.

ACKNOWLEDGMENTS

My thanks to the following men and women who helped with this book:

- All of those at Pauline Books and Media who invested in my book *Theology of the Body Explained*, upon which this short introduction is based.

- Greg Weidman, Nathan West, Matthew Pinto, Dana Vink and Daniel Weiss for reviewing the manuscript and offering helpful suggestions.

- The entire team at Ascension Press for all their work in bringing this book to print.

- Annamarie Adkins, Tracy Moran, Michael Flickinger, Michael Fontecchio, and Michael J. Miller for their editorial and technical assistance.

- Scott Russell and Janene DiBlasio for managing my busy life thus affording me time to write.

- Kinsey Caruth for designing the cover.

- My wife Wendy for her unfailing love and support.

Take the next step in your study of **John Paul II's Theology of the Body**

*I*n my biography of the Pope, I wrote that the theology of the body needs explication for those who aren't specialists in biblical studies, theology, or philosophy. I am delighted that Christopher West has taken up that challenge. With intellectual care, with the experience bred of long years of teaching this material in the classroom and parish, and taking account of his own experiences as a husband and father, Christopher West has put us in his debt by making the "theology of the body" available to a wide and, I hope, appreciative readership.

—From the *Foreword* by George Weigel
Senior Fellow, Ethics and Public Policy Center

Order Today
1-800-376-0520

www.LuminousMedia.org

Start a Study Group

In your home, on your campus, or in your parish.

Introduction to the Theology of the Body

4-talk video series with study guide for participants.

Study Guide

2 Video Set

Created and Redeemed

8-talk video series with study guide for participants.

Study Guide

4 Video Set

Order Today
1-800-376-0520

www.LuminousMedia.org